COLLECTED POEMS: 1937-1962

COLLECTED POEMS: 1937-1962
WINFIELD TOWNLEY SCOTT

THE MACMILLAN COMPANY

NEW YORK 1962

A DIVISION OF THE CROWELL-COLLIER PUBLISHING COMPANY

MACMILLAN NEW YORK, LONDON

To DOUGLAS WINFIELD SCOTT
for his 75th birthday

CONTENTS

COLLECTED POEMS: 1937-1962

TRAMAN, AND WIND THE CLOCK (1937 & 1941)

"Because I helped to wind the clock
I come to hear it strike."
How goes the weather?
—W. B. YEATS

The Spool and the Lighthouse

I saw my gone years turning in the sky—
Brightly away from me and then returning
Returning with vast shapes of mist: I see
Far to the south the sun's bafflement.

Spool of my gathering spawn a patient wheel
Winding my seasons. But the world turns two ways
Therefore, too, the lighthouse that swings
Round into dark, round into dark, round . . .

Always going. The beam of time spins
A halo, and what was dark on earth
Is dark; but what was bright recedes
Always going. And evening tall in the north.

Where Ignorant Armies

The child plays on the sands
Alone, and takes in his hands
Shells, dried stars, sea-grass,
Stones hot with the sun;
And sometimes studies the gulls
Or carefully questions a wave
Or, squat at a troubled pool,
Peers to learn what there was.
Yet turning, will shout and run

3

While foam purrs at his heels:
Then turning will chase it back.
Secure upon beach or rock
He is shrill with delight and daring
Or quiet and staring,
Pleased at the bright confusion
Above his innocent hair
Of birds wild over the sea.
But now he broods by a crab
Busy, as one assured
That afternoon at his back
Is filled with his victory.

Summer Afternoon

Kingdoms in fern guessed, caves beneath moss
Secret but certain; underground den assured
Though lost till tomorrow—all hid in the forest
Immensely ceilinged and mysteriously floored.

The deep path into the beechwood thronged
With the shy intimate sounds of friendly things,
The unseen furred upon the stealthy feet
In dry bracken, the sudden kick of wings,

The shift of a snake gone into leaves, and in
The held hush, farther, the quick plop
Of a wakened frog, and treed above stillness high
And reiterant the bird's cry that could not stop.

Pattern of nervous silence flicked the grass
Splotched with the leafed light where the sky showed

4

Tall, dim—the boy watched it weave
Sleep on the moveless turtle, on the tranced weary toad.

The Temple in the Wilderness

Behold the tiny spinning sphere,
This top gyrating round an invisible
String strung in space, this twinkling
Asterisk, this footnote of naught, this
Item of snow—moist shadow on the enormous
Burning desert of space, and then behold
Your kind that cling here. —Ah, what
Has the vain tongue spoken that is more
Than a thin leaf blown in the forest fire?

O we have built a temple in the wilderness,
Out of dust and tears a mortar become refuge,
The dome besieged with trees and grass.
The tongue has spoken doors and rooms, the mouth
Has shaped the spires and belled them, and behold
The wilderness rings under the encroaching shade,
Rings with this harem of our thought: a dream
More or a dream less that the vain
Tongue, between sleepings, wrought.

Nightmare

The quiet sisters, the solemn brothers, all
Will come and say "You can go in now. It is all

Right for you to go in now." (Though she did not call,
And it is all wrong.) And you will go alone, down the hall
Into the room where she is lying, still and small;
And she and you: each suddenly alone,

(Only this will be a long time from now. Do not
(Think of it now . . . at all.)

Probably it will be dark in the room.
Creviced in the shutters you will see the ore
Of the afternoon sun, waiting uselessly as flowers at a tomb.
You will close the door
To be alone before solitude in the ethered gloom.

(But why do you think of it now? All
(Of this is years away . . . if at all.)

You will raise the sheet,
Curiously seeing the eager feet
Bespelled like the shadowless hands
Carved on the intimate body, grown
Terribly familiar and unknown,
And

(Do not think of it now————)

            watch, unbelieving, the breathlessness
Of the sealed mouth, the empty nostrils . . . hear the bleat
Of the noisy traffic of nothing in the far street . . .
Spy on the incredible strange breast that does not beat;
But hear in your brain the storming whirl of silence.

Enemy lying there
In the friend's body,
Stilling even the illuminate hair,

6

Its dark waves woven inanimate forever.
Answerless, answerless, answerless, the despair
Of your crying hands knuckling Forever.
Peace: fist at your eyes, fingers that tear
Your heart . .

Then they will come, the whispering sisters, the stern
      brothers, all
Into the room, to lead you down the hall,
Out of the room where no one at all will call
You back. No one at all.

Perhaps the Brook

Like music meandering
Cool, thin, lost in grass,
Her laughter, wandering,
Shines, hides, flashes clear,
Leaps at light. Bent to it,
His throat no longer parched
Since his lips went to it,
Catches the singing, holds
Part of the wisdom and
All of the folly now
Charted as his domain.
Wind and sun over this,
Fear not: lean down again.
Thirst alone covers this,
Keeps ice from it.

Truth of This Time

Truth of this time, so proved and undefiled,
The secret of the atom tethered, even
The plotting of our planetary voyage
With prophecy—you mathematic truth:
You shall outlast us and you shall be brave
When we are corollary to the last
Lost undiscoverable fire at the earth's core.

Yet in a ruinous twilight, even you
Our careful calculations shall be told
While watchers of the burning ash of the west
Wait for the glow to cool, as once we stared;
The young men laughing but the children all
Wondering at you, such proud beautiful answers.
For the mythmen have you all in the end,
Whether you speak of light or the end of light
Or the agony of God's Son, it is all one—
A tale for wide-eyed children who must sleep.

A Dream of Ascent from the Sea

At night between the headland and the sea
He stood alone and heard the oncoming waves
Measure a blind way down the guttural rock,
And saw deep in the waters' breaking black
The phosphorescent flowering of their graves.

8

Harsh on his mouth wind pressed the perilous
Salt taste of crystal in seafire bloomed;
He plunged and swam, and all the waters filled
With planetary burning: he grasped and failed,
Returned unsheathed, spent, nude as any man doomed.

Shored fast, face down he gripped the rolling earth,
Felt it turn to the sun; and he turned, and there was
The warm unbespoken light as he stepped
Inland, and stronger on him as he wept
Between the yucca and the wild seagrass.

From General to Particular

This is a long way that we
Have come to face finality.

Since man pushed slime aside
And stood up slowly, feeble-eyed,
All men have died; we have not died.

We went concealed against the sun,
Renewed and guarded and passed on
Eon by eon.

                    The first dawn
Flows in us; even the still, wan
Chaos which light splashed upon:

But this is memory only and
The half-remembered stretched Hand.

Now out of the long secret zone
Of blood and bone
We have escaped, have seen and known
Grass and dirt and tree and stone;

And looked on flesh and loved and lain
Deliriously in flesh again.

From that warm dark you and I
Stand beneath the cold sky
Knowing at last that we shall die.

After the ageless content,
This beautiful, bitter, brief moment.

From anonymous night, the brow
Lifted to all the lights now;

The sleepers waked for martyrdom.
What once we were we shall become.

Second Grade*

Traman remembers the little kid in the schoolyard
Who always stood by the drainpipe till the bell rang.
—Why did you do that? Why did you have to do that?

Yet when the bell rang he was neat in the line,
Out of step usually but first off with his cap.
—Why were you at ease with them only in the schoolroom?

* Pronounce name: tray′ man.

Traman can see him now, tow-head and blue suit,
His skinny black stockings swollen by underwear.
—How in six years of life were you still alien?

Tag swept the corner, tug of war lurched past him,
A fight by the big tree between two eighth grade giants.
—Why did you leave your marbles and aggies at home?

Once in awhile a tough little darkie named Spider
Would go grinning up to him and they would talk about
—What? O, what, what was it, wet grounded leaves?

But most days, punctual, neat, and pale, and silent, he
Stood warily by the drainpipe and spied on the others.
—Who were you? Who were you? cries Traman, partly lying.

Fatty Doran

Mucker Jones began it and all the other boys in the
    schoolyard joined in;
They jumped and jeered around Fatty Doran until they
    mobbed him back to wall.

Fatty, who'd make three of any other twelve-year-old there,
    short or tall,
And who never did anything much but eat candy and
    wait for fun to begin,
Just stood there surprised and uncertain, wondering if it
    might be a joke,
Half ready to smile even when someone said to give his
    old belly a poke.

11

And then Peanut Davis crouched, lunged, kicked Fatty
    sharp on the shin.

The crowd yelled delight. Fatty went white, dumfounded
    and terrified.

In excited fellowship the kids pranced, advanced, called
    him pot-face, fat-ass,
Powder-puff, pink-snot, yanked his sweater and pants,
    said Let's see what he has,
Old mamma's titty-boy; and though Fatty flailed the air
    and for a minute tried
To beat the kids off he faltered, stared, his mouth
    trembled and then he cried.

Mucker said Cry-baby, and a few guffawed to see the big
    boy sob and choke
Huddled to the wall and towering over them.

                                        Windy Weyman spoke—
Said to leave Fatty alone,—and it was quiet and some
    moved off as though to be rid
Of any notion that what had gone on had been any concern
    of theirs

Later at recess, deeply casual, several encountered Fatty
    singly or in pairs
And whether it was marbles or scrub-ball or swimming or
    hunting sweet-fern to smoke
They hoped he had time for, Fatty grinned shyly and
    told them sure he did.

Mucker Jones

Small, yellow, dirt-scaled, odorous,
Fifteen, and thin as he was sly,
Mucker Jones scuffed to his chair
An aged rebellion in his eye.

A sullen arrogance became
His secret face, until his lips
Too small and sharp for any child's
Drew down as if expecting whips.

There was a wisdom to his filth—
That accurate coverage of his mind—
Too wise for others of his years
And foreign to the schoolroom kind.

Recess time, he would often hint
Of fierce unhappy joys he hid,
Of Reba, Sadie, and the barn
Behind his house, and what they did.

He may have lied about his drink;
His cigarette was real enough—
His hands stained with the fact of that,
His flat lungs laboring to cough.

But even if he looked beaten, caught,
The other children always paid
Homage to unsurrendering hate,
The truant and the renegade.

Glory unsullied wholly came
When his spit, far from where he stood,
Examined by the admirers, vouched
That he spoke truth, that it was blood.

Sunday Night

Darrah was there, his pinwheel talk
Sizzling and sputtering round the room,
Big Dutch ponderous by the lamp
And Cary wistful in the gloom:

Fireworks and blunderbuss
And exuberant chameleon
Performed a dance on beer and smoke
From Halifax to Helicon;

While Traman, indeterminate
Between the ceiling and the floor,
Reclined upon a cloud of ease
Or floated to the privy door,

Wherefrom emerging into sound
Of revelry he drank again—
No fiery pillar certainly
But still, one of four gentlemen

Who arduously prophesied
The ways of their indigenous trees
Which rising from familiar soil
Should pattern heaven's American frieze.

And whether in such boughs should swing
Testaments, angels, orioles,
Became less moment than the yeast
Expanding gently in their souls,

And quite forgotten when with last
Descent through ale and cold cigars,
Traman, in the wintry night,
Strode home hearing the morning stars.

The Island in the Sea

(*All the steam in the world could not, like the Virgin,
build Chartres.—Henry Adams*)

Nevertheless—

Now being done with twenty-three of his years,
Traman has fifty left with which to die.
He sorts the twenty-three skeletons,
Peers into each enigmatic eye,
Tests suture and socket; fears
Losing any sun still stored
In skull or joint if he let it lie.

His intent swerves: he rides into graves and
Over graves, cuddling a bone or powdering the air.
He has no compass for hope nor map of despair.
One thing alone he knows as certain and sure—
The nightingales are dead in Union Square.

But staring from the Battery,
Traman pursues his usual dream
Begotten by the river on the sea—
Carefully building a Chartres of his own,
Amassing this coral, slow spawn of his bone.
It burns in the sea with a terrible private noise,
The clash of assembled structure that will be
His breath and death together, its stern poise
Compounded of his bodies. He imagines
Strange engines are at work with him, and tides
Fall back even now from it, are shifted;
That at last in its final perfection, lifted
Through the seething water, it will stand
With nightingales and Chartres on either hand
And triumphant trumpets blowing from the sea.

The Fish Sonata

Having banged the piano too hard
Traman turned and looked around
And seeing his friends assembled said
"To hell with that Almighty sound.

It is," he said,—with something still
Resembling an enlarging air—
"My *Fish Sonata*: oversoul
Voyaging an underworld despair.

While less than panoramic zeal
Eliminated vaster plans,
I found myself intrigued between
The tadpoles and leviathans;—

Then plumped for giants. And you've heard:
A mackerel music round the whales.
There's nothing drier than dried fish.
Drink up, and I will practise scales."

And Traman thereupon swung back
And found the keys as clean and fair;
And, thinking over what he'd said,
Wished his friends were really there.

Easy Nakedness

for Jeff

Wet-foot-printed our separate paths
Cross into the room from morning baths
(Traman thus of Kurt one day)
And we towel, each a little away
From the window where the sun floods in
But near enough for sun on skin;
Stay, careful of peace, within the shaft.
Your smoke escalates on the bright draught
As the light itself ascends, descends.
We are young men and old friends;
Stripped, you are casual and I
Am at last not reticently shy,
You and the sun together release
A thaw—I grow consciously at ease.
We are different flesh, no doubt of that;
Without affliction you favor fat
But I cling to bone and a stomach flat
As a boy's and very skinny arms.
This body's not one of my major charms

Whereas, I imagine, Marges and Megs
Have pleasure 'round your stolid legs.
I'm pale, of course, you ten shades browner
Yet with a less savage fur
Darkening toward navel and over chest.
Your head firmer—not large for the rest;
The sex franker and heavier,
And one wildness: a black lozenger
Of hairy mole on the buttock-girth.
My strawberry knee-splotch from birth
Is nothing to match that Satanic brand.
I watch your cigarette and the hand
Working it—fingers feminine,
Fine: one feature I'm stronger in.
—If I could give up verse for paint
As I like to think I could, past restraint
Of ignorance and the days I moan
To shine at piano or sculpt stone,
I would get us fixed as here—the one
Dark, the other light in the sun
And stark bare for good, the two
At the lazy morning talk we do;
Lines simple, no outer comment,
The whole bulged with such yellow content
No critic need ask what the thing meant.

Dream Penny in the Slot at 6 A.M.

Dreaming, he turns the crank to wind her
Through his own eyes that he looks into, and
The girl moves toward him through going mist
Nearer and clearer as though through unwound days and hours
Slowly; and veil after veil slides apart and behind her,

Veils moving over and away from her, ankle and wrist
Breaking the dark dominion. Then the spotlights find her;
Traman sees the long aisle of crushed flowers behind her,
How even now she stands in trampled flowers.

But then he looks again through the small
Slot; keeps busy with the crank's turning (tired)
And sees that it is not flowers at all:
Running in flickers of light at him (not
tired) she kicks the fallen leaves in the road hollows:
Hot against him now, laughing (this is fun),
Her hair sweet like grass that lies a day in the sun.
She runs away from him. He follows

We will lie in the sun, Traman yells at her. He shouts
We will lie a long time in the sun. But then he sees
The sun going down between his knees: so he props
Her, very solemn, against a haystack and whispers
That the sun isn't going at all down, down now, anytime ever
     down; and the sun, sure enough, stops.

Something plops.
Light flares. Traman is alone, blind,
And will not remember how he got out of the place
Nor clearly what happened; nor will he greatly mind,
Being stunned and bewildered, his ears ringing with the terrible
     thunder of all those suddenly collected veils fallen between
     him and her beautiful face

Backdrop for This Particular Stage

Sunset crayon-scribbles over alphabet of stone,
Phrase of stone, interwoven syllables and knitted

19

Blocks of stone, flying, upward flying with strict
Precision; fabric of cement and steel, wedges
Driven in the breaking sky, the jumbled skies which are
All at once nailed still by the evening star.

And already the electric stars, stemming from earth,
Anticipate the evening: the red sky hangs silent
Behind these twinkling towers, twittering towers that tremble
Above the horns and the thundering traffic, the confused
Whistles under the bridge whose sweeping wires
Are vibrant with the playing lights in the ascending spires.

O terrible thrust skyward, carefully daring leap
Of baffled stone, the patient letter-blocks erected, leaving
The sentences all unfinished, the alphabet scrambled
Dizzily, pathetically in the air; the anxious pride that laughs
Like a nervous boy attaining a higher limb, looking down afraid,
Then looking out still, amazed, alone, in the dignified shade.

Or he is dreaming, the dissatisfied with mountains, and rearing
His own, more splendid, more beautiful, more meaningless.
He can build only as far as he can scale untoppling,
Erecting the ever unfinished word, the ever broken phrase—
His image and his image of himself, strong and undone,
Thought Traman, and watched these towers lifting slowly against
    the sun.

Daily Birth

Cock of dawn, whose turgid cry
Beats on an unurbanized
Savage arch past Traman's head,
Sling a glittering bridge toward sleep.—

Warned, awaking, Traman stirs
And feels his flesh come over him,
Harden on his length and claim
His mind, teasing it into light.

The sun's his enemy awhile.
This is a sweet—a sweet poison
Loads his limbs; and he resists
That clutch of day, street, folk.

The pattern forms: the consequent,
Need, alliance; the demand
That he invest his crocodile,
Worry the swamp and smile through reeds.

Curled in the warm womb of bed,
Tightly he sucks oblivion
Where the uncensored nightingales
Hymn among shades unrisen sun.—

Cock of dawn, whose swollen beak
Stammers crescent urgencies
Blatant in the unshamed air,
Strut the excremental hill.

—And he is caught in the slow ache
Emergent with expiring dreams
And facefirst twists up to the light
Body unwilling for its chains.

Yet soon grown used, and not unpleased
With so much morning on his bed,
He stands, he walks in light, he bows
His head to brush his teeth again.

Traman Walks to Work

1.

Twenty-ninth winter—Traman faces
More than loss of leaves and coming of snow.
It was always so. It was always something
He had or had not to make him grieve.
Warts, then pimples, and now thinning hair
Seem all his history; and he regards
The waning of his third decade by the light
Of 6 A.M., and that is mostly dark;
Morning uncertain still save for its cold.

Traman walks to work by windy streets,
By dumb houses and the fluttering lights
That rattle out in the day dusk. Traman
Half mad yet from night insanity,
His dreams' lamentations and fornications;
His brain spins, spins. He confronts
His possible failure, hates his hopes,
Cartwheels into town: over and over,
Triumph disaster triumph disaster.

Will the days go wild at last, the dawn
Crumple and the city freeze
Into this lightless sleep and Traman
Walk toward bread and butter hopelessly
Under a larger failure than his own?
He thinks nothing now: the pavement
Hard and cold at his heels, but behind him
The only planet he knows the name of
—Venus—rising and burning.

2.

Walking out in morning snow
Traman has devised a game.
By taking steps longer and slow
He can make his stride the same
As someone's, whose he doesn't know,
That came this way before he came.

He lunges patiently and long
A block or so, and then gives out—
His balance wasn't ever strong,
Now knee muscles all in doubt
He wavers in his thought or song
And stops to breathe and look about.

Between the rabble of the trees
The sky shines like a kindly fate;
Traman, in snow up to his knees,
Learns not to labor but to wait.
With only his own legs to please
He goes again—goes his own gait.

Five for the Grace of Man

1

See this air, how empty it is of angels
Over O'Ryan's barroom. The bum thrown out
Shoulders the sidewalk, pushes it away,
His hat rolling and his baldspot gleaming
Under the rain and under O'Ryan's lights.

I watch from the opposite curb and do not know
Why the old boy was booted; he got the air
Maybe because his nickels were gone, maybe
Because he tried to cadge from those who now
Bar the door and laugh when he tries to enter.

See him there, arms at surrender pressing
Against the mucky glass, the jeering faces
He touches but cannot touch: they're in, he's out;
—Like a child's game: only he's sort of old,
And drunk and broke, alone, the game turned real.

2

A clock strikes midnight and the street lamp burps,
Calms and hums again and tries to light
This soot-clogged, rain-flecked, unangelic air.
I lean on the iron rails above the river
But stare at the emptied road: bar closed, whores home.

I am always waiting for something I do not know
And may as well wait here as any place.
Back streets are better than main streets for waiting
And night is better than day, being privater,
Vacated by all I am not looking for.

As the world pitches east I'm on a line
Between O'Ryan's darkened bar and the light
Storm-hid but drumming of the star Orion.
Romantic—Classic, and me in the middle:
Not much, but all there seems to be tonight.

3

I am getting in the habit of hunting graveyards
In search of the living moments; as though the air
Emptied in fact of mortal flesh, the ground

That took it in might hold the germ of it
And I knowing it was here, know what was here.

See this air, how empty it is of angels,
And how the sunlight falling on the names,
Dates, new masonic emblems and old cherubs
Holds with the calm of daylight on the dead
The possible answer to all our separateness.

As though at the extremes of alienation,
My parenthetical hands training my face,
I peer into the house of this completion
To know my meaning, even to find whether
All men are brothers or all my enemies.

4

How shall I ever come to any good
And get my works in schoolbooks if I use
The rude word here and there, but how shall I
Let you know me if I bequeath you only
The several photographs, the family letters?

There is no image of a tired mind
Tired of its own vanity for fame.
I turn in the comfort of the midnight rain
And as much for pleasure as necessity
Piss in the river beyond O'Ryan's bar.

5

The night is common with fatigue and rain,
With one o'clock and far freights, then with trucks
Roaring toward the Post Road, then my walk
Resuming sound; trees shake out the shower,
I get a second wind, and the sky's clearing.

I know men happy drunk, some happy sober,
And some that, drunk or sober, are alone—
Rather, know they are alone. Myself,
I'm occupied investigating angels
Though there's a power of prose draining the air.

Poetry, I hear, is to be read aloud—
Like epitaphs by cemetery strollers
On Sunday afternoons? There's always Monday,
Which interests me more: I want an angel
Easy in the house on weekday mornings.

I want the separated hand and voice
Brought commonly together: flesh and word
Concerning whether stars or buttonholes
Only together can come through night and death
And move with morning light as with massed liberating wings.

Landscape as Metal and Flowers

All over America railroads ride through roses.

I should explain this is thoroughly a matter of fact.
Wherever sandy earth is piled to make a road for train tracks
The banks on either side are covered with wild, sweet
Pink rambler roses: not because roses are pretty
But because ramblers grow in cheap soil and will hold
The banks firm against rain—therefore the railroad roses.

All over America the steel-supporting flowers,
Sometimes at village depots covering the shingled station,
Sometimes embracing watertanks, but mostly endless tendrils

Out of which locomotives and pullmans flash the morning—
And tunnels the other way into whose firm, sweet evening
The whistle fades, dragging freight cars, day coaches and the
caboose.

Out of Season: Newport

Always when autumn comes on and the Saturday morning rains
I remember hunting horsechestnuts. It is the best weather.
I remember a particular time, my sister and I
Setting out with the cart and a burlap bag toward the rich section.

It is the best weather for the rain was heavy at night, the wind
Chilled the dark day, spattered harbor mist through the town trees;
And up the street we trudged toward the Avenue
Of great lawns and chestnuts and a marvelous harvest.

It was something for nothing, I guess. A few horsechestnuts
And strings to toss them appeased my generation, but I
For no utilitarian reason coveted cartloads—
And there they glistened by hundreds in the rain-thick grass,

Bounced on the gravel walk, into the gutter leaves, shining
Out of their leathery husks, or half out, and yet more beyond
The long fence made of two iron pipes horizontal
Through green wooden posts carved with acorn tops.

It was some minutes after I had dared crawl through
And had raced back and forth to the burlap bag which my sister
Sustained half full by strength of herself and the fence
I saw the rich boy and girl in the window laughing at us.

The house was so far across the lawn that maybe
They will not see my face redden, my hands' uncertain shame.
As if I had not been observed I pick up three more
And show as I leave through the rails that this special work

I've reason to do has been done sufficiently here.
"Let's go home now." And Jeannette says, "I'll help pull."
And we start dragging the cart very carefully down the street.
Anyone seeing us can see what we're doing is all right to do.

Indian Summer—Buffalo Summer

Opened like a big new colored-picture book,
The morning took us early with the summer wind
Coming over the streets and yards from the harbor.

There was no game good enough for that morning.
By 10 o'clock my mother put on her new shirtwaist
And Aunt Essie was there in her black hat with the cherries.

I ran ahead of them, all the way to the corner
Clutching my cap pistol, ran out of the sun
And climbed a bench in the little park under the walnuts.

It must have been time: on the curbs all fathers and mothers,
Even Miss Pitman and her cane, old Mr. Kaull and his pipe,
Baby Shea, the big policeman, in the middle of Broadway.

Just then I caught my sister and pulled out her hair-ribbon.
O then we stood still and amazed, hearing far off
The sweet incredible fife, the murmur of coming drums.

28

Every now and then a cop on a motorcycle.
But at last over the dust, out of the shade and light,
The Indians rode before us their arrogant horses.

Ah I had no genuine breath for such word made flesh—
The brown torsos, cheekbones, streaked with warpaint,
The head-dresses blowing wide like unfurled turkeys.

Then came the squaws, then came the little Indians,
And cages with buffaloes, wolves, hyenas, coyotes,
An ancient stagecoach waddling, and then the scouts—

The scouts with lashed-leather gloves and buckskin jackets,
Bearing their rifles bravely across their knees,
And then just behind them an old man in an open carriage.

Old, old Buffalo Bill, bowing and smiling,
Lifting his hat from his long white hair, and riding
Right up Broadway in a little yellow-wheeled cart.

We'll All Feel Gay

Even along the railway platform it was spring
And my uncle was coming on the noon train, back from the war.
I was nine that month. I had a new cap and no coat.
We walked around, my grandfather and I, and watched the tracks.

The tracks slid shining and quiet with the warm sun
And the station stayed very still. Hunched on the baggage-wagon
The blue baggageman smoked his pipe, said "How-do, Mr. Scott,"
And my grandfather said "My son is getting back on this train";

And then it was coming. We stopped walking and listened, and
    then
The engine roared at the turn and raced at us and darkened
The whole station and shook it and I yelled "There he is!"
He leaned on a cane and stood very big in his khaki.

So we all sort of shook hands and the other people
Laughed and waved as they went by, and my uncle said
"Well, how's the new bus?" as we climbed into the
1919 green Cadillac touring.

We drove past the ballfield and up Pelham Street,
And they talked about the car, and into Spring Street and Broad-
    way,
And not about the hospital or the Argonne or France or
The Botches or anything like that; and my uncle

Looked at all the stores we went past—my grandfather's too,
With the seed packages bright in the window, and outside
Gilt-and-green lawn-mowers in a row where the elm trees
Cast a thin shade leafing across the brick sidewalk.

We drove through Friendship to our Street; my grandfather
Said the paint department yes should be moved, as they walked
Up the steps; but my uncle's cane crashed to the floor
And he was running all the way to the door where my grandmother
    stood.

Shoetown

I think every day of the city where I was a boy—
I remember all of it, too: not only the river road

Flanked with autumnal color nor gold-leaf water
Nor the slow hills around, nor the smoke of thin spring—

That was after the war; money was easy, and everyone
Kept up his lawn in summer evenings and went
For a ride in the new car and was mostly young—even
The Armenian and Italian shoestitchers got fur coats

And the Jews were buying up Main Street while the Yankees
Moved over a block or two, I remember; and the first to have
Radios—the Irish—bought big ones on installment.
The noise of things broken on the air began then

And in the daylight-saving we kids sat under neighbors' windows
To listen to the crackling notes of speech or jazz; and "Static," we
        said,
Sucking grass or wrestling or watching the fireflies
Bewildered over the new cellar holes in the near fields.

I remember the small bare bottoms of the kids I knew—
How they used to plunge and disappear and bounce out
Shining in the brown river in the afternoons, even until
The leaves were coming down brown and gold—O gosh, yes!

And that was not longer than ten—fifteen years ago
Before everything began to close up; the factories shut,
Houses unpainted along the frost-split streets and no
Macadam nor paint thought of, with clothes color-sad;

Mr. Forrester shot himself at the Bank; Benny Goldstein
Lost his apartment houses; the stores took back the Armenians'
Rugs and furniture; the Italians moved on with the shops; the
Irish got on relief, and the Yankees voted for Hoover.

Two chickens in the pot around the corner.
"Static—static—static": and all the while everywhere
Coming down the river and over the trees and up the steps and
    under
The evening grass, the no-sound of everything breaking in air.

Grant Wood's American Landscape

This is not real: this is the shape of a dream spun
By a strong man with X-ray eyes that see
Through enormous planes of sun the design that no sun
Can reveal clear any more: at best we remember vaguely, seeing
These mornings these afternoons these clean
Men and women like a child's long day in the sunlight that no one
Remembers any more: it is drenched, it is gone in the sun.

But this is the way it was, and this is the way the old men
Dreamed it in the beginning: proud land with no end:
Patterned with quilt-like honesty and fenced
For honesty but not to keep anyone out or anyone in:
Patterned with the sure line of the plow and the bright line
Of the corn and the colors of soil changing
As far as the sky in the shadows of wind.

                              And this
Is the way it was, but this is not real: these houses white,
Precise, angled with safety, islanded in the rich grass:
These people going and coming at fruitful chores: these barns'
    weight
Solid beyond the fat-cheeked trees in the sun: and the land in the
    sun
Immensely stretched and never too much to roll and reach

Farther than we could say, and everywhere such strictness
Set upon luxury justly: these tracks of the share and the wheel
Show that the men are sure and wise in their labor, they go back
And forth too clean and sure: they are not real.

There is too much sun. There is too much peace.

Monuments of War

Monuments of war, where the green branch
Over the Common sheds dappled shade,
Of shaped clay make immortal guardians
(So was the intent) of this ripe peace,
Upon the pedestal in fixed parade
A village testimonial to art and arms.

This ancient youth turned stone becomes
Sentry of seasons; unrelieved and calm
Above piled cannon shot and metal wreath
He bears his solid image of a gun
As though far off under the sky his drums
Thunder through fields reverberant with graves.

The slow and hollow signals of the dead
Sound on stone ears alone: they make no more
Than unheard fragrance moving here among
Renewing trees whose immaculate June
Stares the air to a soft sleep of gold
Reward for living.

        Yet still the plugged cannon
Defends the empty Square and the dispersed

Dust of a generation in whose guise
This eyeless statue stands memorial
Gifted for lengthier decay, that all
May cherish how the lost victorious young
Sprung early this green victory of grass.

Fine Morning

It is a fine May morning. Professor Arturo Esposito observes it
    shyly at 8:40 in Providence, R.I.,
By leaving hatless for the campus and neglecting
His little twisted cigar. All this he recognizes. Or, spring is strange
    everywhere
So even here it is meeting with a beautiful woman, new and
    (perhaps) unattached.

Well, he is a 50-year-old exile with not enough hair and too much
    belly, he says,
Remarking on the day to his colleague, Vicquart, whom he en-
    counters at the corner.
Together they go up the hill along maple-dappled brick wall and
    walk,
The meeting-house steeple shining below them. "Look," says
    Esposito: "even the pigeon shines."

M. Louis Vicquart, recently of Sorbonne and a discovered Jewish
    strain, is young,
Is serious, is gentle, is correct, is immaculate in morning clothes
    and a cane.
Esposito likes to make him laugh; Vicquart very earnestly wants
    to oblige;
And though the Frenchman is tense as his wing-collar, and the
    Italian's gaiety is unpressed,

34

Still, everything is O.K. Vicquart says always by way of applause:
    "That is O.K."
"Love moves the sun, et cetera, and only geese get moved by
    goose-step—eh?
Imagine a General marching past those lilacs on such a morning,
    Vicquart.
Flowers are just pretty—eh?—but why do they make so much
    else seem half-wit?"

"That is O.K." says Vicquart. "O.K., O.K., O.K.," sing all the
    robins in international English.
The sun shines and the robins sing: and even three blocks away
    at the corner by the tulip tree,
Because old Professor Heinrich Werner, bent over his beard and
    pipe, pauses
Much longer than traffic requires on Angell Street. "Everything
    smells good," he says aloud.

"It is not Heidelberg, but—no: It is not Heidelberg and
Everything smells good." And it does two blocks the other side
    of the campus where
Vladimir Samolkin, the round, the gleaming, the Russian mathe-
    matician, hums a bar
From last night's Bach, smiles blindly past wistaria as if breathing
    Bach alone.

So there they come: Esposito, Vicquart, Werner, Samolkin, into
    the elm-laved campus sun,
As the bell starts for 9-o'clocks, and students leave the paths to
    cross wet grass,
And all the dormitory windows are open, and voices loafing on
    the early breeze,
Classroom doors all open. All O.K. All on a fine May morning.

So

So it isn't a newsreel anymore, but war.
The lights go on, the theater's gone, the screen dissolves.
But battleships, bombers are all there as before
But real, and the street shakes and the sky revolves.

So it isn't a game either, with a possible score
Of 12 to 6 or even 12 to 0;
And the other side happy and your side sore
But peanuts for everyone. But an end of winning.

It is you, that had read about cancer now and then,
Leaving the doctor's office trying to know
It is I. How can it? How long? It is I. When?
—Not somebody else in the papers: too bad but so.

It is so, and what you can do about it is nothing.
Fight: it is here. Do not fight: it is here.
Some will be dead sooner, and some surviving
Awhile to inherit blood and the seed of murder.

Spain Once Danced

I remember La Argentina, the beautiful dancer
Who died suddenly: her heart grown big felled her.
She was a beautiful dancer, a dark dancer.
She would not be there: stage, a widening silence.

Then in the hidden wings the slow stir, the whispered
Chuckle, the sly castanets beginning beginning.
Yes? Not yet, no. Yes. The mischievous clock
Ticked again: tried: rustled: stammered, ran wild,
And she swept there upon the incredible air
With the great skirt of her dancing spinning the light,
And theater whirling under the Spanish music
Of her swift dancing. Spill, cascade, fountain,
Flicking clutter of flowers, her fingers' laughter.

Crocus Air

Let the crocus air invoke spring.
Gardens are not impossible.
Sun steams on the roofs where
Snow has hung.

The new-straw color of sun,
The sky's thawed blue.
Simple is grass and simple
The dandelion.

I believe in the circling wall,
I believe in the orchard lawn
For you and me and the child,
Though nothing is here at all.

The Stake

Hope that is hot: desire heats the needle
That roves before me searching the arctic star.

(This is music: listen, will be enough.)
And the prong in the glass spins dizzy with metal.

This is my history, yet not enough: yet
Not altogether blind though I have turned
Vaguely in many alleys where old clothes
Stank on the lines between the tenements.

And I have groped the barren valley, nights
After the hurricane: sloped houses, trees
Pitched over the strewn stone, and bones
Thrust out of stormy graves and yet silent.

(Yet this is music.) There is a sea-way
And a ship lolling and diving, the mast
Ringing all quarters of the sky—a halo
Of horizon, a hoop-rolling of hemispheres.

Yet in my own street often a lost man
I walk and walk, coming and going daily
Between all my uncertainties: I talk
Much to myself, having no listeners.

I have no loneliness beyond desire
That keeps me lonely: no knowledge
Over curb, fence and lamppost, corner,
The hot ignorance of my gathering blood.

I would know things relevant to this polar stake,
This mast, this pylon of a landing field
I soar at endlessly with roaring hope;
Or in my own house stretch shaking fingers.

Totem scarred with legendary faces
Coloring the icy beach of the far rocks;

And flesh the night lengthens and hardens from me
Jutting cockalorum at the sun:

God in the pole, god in the body axis
Reared in this room, or staked in a swaying north
Or drawing me inward to a central tower:
On that, my crucifixion or my flag.

Old Talk

His mind dove down from the stars and curled in his head.
It said, We cannot know what we have no sense to know.
And the body said, Be still, take it easy; it is better so.

Mind was dizzy with space where it curved and sped
And it lay still to get warm. The body said, You are cold;
And the mind, Let us stay close together and be comforted.

The body went walking, went walking, went walking,
More or less alone the body went walking: took the tube
Rode up and down in steel, shot dry under river, felt old.

Where were you all day? asked the body; and the mind
Woke as the body would have gone to sleep. Left behind:
One of us, it said, always goes too high, or too deep.

Then while the night tossed, the cricket-mind sang and sang:
Remember—it sang—when the world was snug and small
With nothing all the morning for you to do but toss a ball
Against a sunlighted wall.
                              And there was one street,
One house and yard changing color, spring and fall.
—Yes, said the body, that was a sweet time and neat; but.

Then the mind said, Always too high now or too deep.
What can we do about it now we're together? the body said.
Well, if it's peace we want, we can always go to sleep.

So for a time the stars flowed on, easy and unbeheld.
Even the mind drowsed in the slack, forgotten head.
Neither ever knew, in the morning, which of them rebelled.

Street Looks

That street-glance of human diffidence, indifference, even of scorn.
Will in all kinds of weather sometimes mutually fail: a face
Confronts me, really returns my real look that I had not thought
    to give:
A knowledge, a questioning, a hope dilate the air happily,
A mask dissolves, and someone strange and new and known looks
    and goes by.
Why did I not say to her: Wait—you are beautiful, and who are
    you?
And to that ragged young man whose home was not anywhere
    here:
Wait—what are you—what were you going to say?
                          And make
A smaller hell, a warmer brighter hell here in hell.

The House

When will violence shake, when break me—
Make me at last cry out? What loss

Heavy to crack my personal sky? What
Failure darken to bring me staring?
What good thing, evil thing—come either—
Split me and let the frozen blood?

I hear beneath the wind, beneath
The leaves' skating on the ground,
My ancestors' hair growing, whispering,
A tide out of the old men's skulls:
Think it flicks me, teases my fingers,
Writhes at my ankles, rejoices and grieves.

I walk up the stairs and walk down,
Hear news of murder and confront my death:
Death—death—death of love—a shape
Rocking a chair somewhere in this house.
Mirrors everywhere reflect me here
Going from room to room, lest I decrease.

If smaller, harder—then for what escape?
The sky grinning through the window
The hair furtive under the door—
What damnation damns me! And you:
I might speak of it and find it with you.
The air chokes my open mouth.

Haunted then? caught? snagged up
In a web of lies? dreaming?
Many questions for you and no answers.
I dare not and I know not what I dare not.
Then this is mad? and black blood wants peace?
Come peace. Come violence. Come violent peace.

Swedish Angel

The Swedish angel is nine inches high and shaped all of blond
  straw.
All of blond straw is her little body and her great seven-inch
  wings.
Her small head is of painted wood and she stands in a slim wood
  base.
Shining and shining in the Christmas candles, shines her golden
  halo.

Even all round her is a kind of shining, circle on circle, because
She has—as if—lighted upon a round lake of clear glass
Surrounded by ground-pine and red berries which gleam also
In the candlelight that moves on her stilled blond wings.

In this immaculate doll of heaven has been conceived, as though
No hands had shaped her, an uninvented innocence bequeathing
  grace
Ring upon ring in halos all around her, and not remote nor kind
But only there, dispensing of all the brought light a total larger
  light.

Even now her wings have assumed such shields of glory and the
  pool beneath
Wheels with such wreaths of shining, the room is gathered and
  filled
By her tall and burning stillness and, an actual angel, her suspension wars
For a whole minute against all the dark, as if I were a child.

Natural Causes

I died, and they looked in my head: 2 plus 2
Equals 3, and the faucet that dripped unmended,
The cracked gauge on the furnace, the fraying cuff

—These they found, and ten unpaid bills, and
2 plus 2 equals 2: certain marbles I lost as a child
Through a boardwalk; a flamingo feather I kept

For years but had nothing it went with, a
Foreign thing; one copy of *Huck Finn*; 20 boxes
Of empty pay envelopes, and a pseudo-sheep diploma.

There was talk of heartbreak via nerves; matter of fact
The autopsy was notable for the splendid tone of the aorta,
And legally bled I lay there in my own ice water.

But they missed the scrap of film—and anyway
Had no unionman, nor a projector if they'd had—
Of the girl running toward me forever through the
    cloversunned field.

Day-End

Watching the sunlight fail along the wall
My shadow taller than I shall be tall
Thins and dissolves and is nothing at all.

Now like an arm whose signal is release
Now like a small hand moving across my knees
The light touches and rests and goes like peace.

And leaves a furry blurr, a patch of warm shade
Laid on me lingering as though it said
That of such light such shadow of dark is made.

I turn in the evening dusk and go to the window
To the clear falls of the birds singing and the slow
Smell of tidal darkness, the rising shadow.

Slowly the rain begins, scattered and small.

On the Brief Disinterment at London, 1938, of the Bones of Possibly Michael Drayton, Poet, by Certain Theorists in Search of the Disproof of William Shakspere in the Grave of Edmund Spenser

Three hundred years of night may utter gems;
But Michael Drayton's bones are the rubbish of night,
By accident, from an old bed of the Thames,
Hauled back to the light.

So. And a man twice to be brought to the air?
Yet this time not to breathe or know nor cry of it.
Nor see sun in the street, girls walking there,
Nor to die of it.

Impersonal light—impersonal bone,
No look of luck between light and the leer
Of this insane foreign nonsense that had known
Sense once native here.

To touch the skull and the fragment of the hand
A twentieth century scavenged and brought up
As from a search for wine a clot of sand
And a broken cup.

Since there's no help, come let us kiss and part.
Lean through three centuries and learn to sever
The skeleton from the sun, dead bones from art.
Shake hands forever.

Dublin, 1938

Old Yeats at the Abbey Theatre,
Face wounded by his dark eyeglass,
Stood tall and grave before
The blasts of young applause:
That only the words counted—
All else waste and a weariness.
Nevertheless the man stood,
Being called: the minute
Testified with the impermanent body,
There, which had borne in itself
Singular victory someway partly ours.

Dryburgh Abbey

The stone walls, roofless and broken, lie open in the light.
In the corridors and chancels the grass grows, and the sun
    stands.

At the place of the high altar, rock is hairy with ivy
And the moss moves with shadow and shine over, over,
Soft on the column drums. Church hewn by hands,
In a hundred and a hundred and a hundred and a hundred years
Lies split, stilled, ended, laced to the earth, beautiful.
Beautiful and quiet because it is broken, roofless, sundered.

We are not mocked; this is true, means what it means—
The larks fly through these upright Gothic ribs,
This skeleton the sun reclaims, the grass makes good.

Empire's Child

What man shall praise Scotland
With uncorrupted talk?
To find what place to stand
Between the shadow and rock
And raise the native wand?

He hears the loch-side song
The chaffinch-whirling tree,
And the brooks outflung
From the cliff in this country;
They murmur the local tongue.

The men who scuff the dust
In the roads under the hills,
For bread of speech have crust
That breaks in the mouth and fells
The echo of music lost.

The penny and song are one,
And lost in a land that grieves—
Unutterable, foresworn;
The mountains, massive graves
Of the kings that were not born.

Menhir

Whether for death or love, it stood
On the sparse ridge above the wood—
The monolith, the menhir stone.
Enormous muscled rock, not grown
In that plain country, twice man-high,
Buried in ground, impaled the sky:
Became the axle on which spun
Earth two ways around the sun.
Singular and left alone,
Whether for love or death, the stone
Marked that waste field dedicate
To something that was man's estate:
A violence upon that ground
While earth whirled dizzily around;
A violence which, though spent at length,
One morning more regathered strength
And thus to signalize the intent
Dragged and raised this monument
That universe and world, made sure
By whatever it was men met here for,
Might turn on that one victory more.

Letters of Our Travel

Wake and gull wake ship-drawn behind us
Might be in the wing-filled wind the cast shreds
Of diaries, letters of our travel, a fluttered farewell
Strewn, tossed to the green banks: goodbye, England;

But are feathers and foam shadowed or shining
Streaming from the high shore till night falls, the soft cliffs
Descend the east dark and the stars from the North Sea
Rash sky, condense to mist over moorlands, over Scotland,

Over the lowland borders, my great-grandfathers' graves
Deep and hollow in the old island, and my name left there.
At the ship's rail edging the wall of midnight, wonder
Of time returns, blood memory and mysterious knowledge

Wound with sea-throb and grieving the westward journey,
Mindful of turf banks delved by the gnarling road,
Thatch out of ground arrayed in the late light evening
In the ancient dusk the flocks of skylarks flying;

Strange over the once wave-wakened now tide-lulled island
How from generations of man the land takes its age-weight.
All walking against the sun is dream; I turn with time
And ascend the night toward morning in the west.

Elegy for Robinson

His Word

Measure my days with the wind,
With wings on the sea, with a stone
Turned over and the sun on the dark earth,
And a veil of many voices:
                    the face
Drawn slenderly on the sky;
The soundless endless falling of the leaves
Never obscures the wondering gaze.

Measure my hand lest, not being
A palm of dust only, it may hold
Tenderly the untiring heart,
Naked out of the body and alive.

Scorn that was stern as love—both
These I meant to bear in a barren day;
Measure my hours that were a single hour,
The love and the scorn, singular.

In New York: 1900

What has he got? said everyone hurrying in the opposite direction.
Bubble-work, bubble-work, said the sewer.
Where is he getting? said Dear Friend on the other corner.
It'll be me or you, said gaslight to river, and the snow
      came down between;

49

Snow came down—the gathering shreds of shadow—
And filled the street with a soft silt.
He's got secrets, said the street: He's got secrets.

Blurred under the blown light the man's footmarks in the snow
Are the only prints in the street this night: they turn
Up steps to the rooming-house.
                                        Inside, he plods stairs
Behind him. He has a key in his pocket. He has a door
That fits the key for the time being; he unlocks and closes to
The bed, the chair, the mirrorless bureau, books and stove;
To his tall familiar shadow flat against the wall.

Only along the window is the snow vocal—beyond,
Behind him, there are miles of silent snow
Covering the night northward, and to the east falling
Blind on the sea slung coldly out from Maine;
And inland snow that even in his mind now falls
With sounds no word is quiet enough to say
What driven peace invades the coming morning
That it may rise from requiem and be strong; and rise
Less for itself than for the dead and the unborn.
                                        And yet
This incurving day must be the sum of all: again: again;
Spent, misspent, the defeat, resolve and pride,
The single purpose like a ravenous scourge—these are the sun
Heating terrifically the slavish brain; and these the only one.

In the slow turning mirrors of his mind he sees
His eyes bemused in their long private research, looking
Deep in to see far out: even that town he must forsake—
Forsaken: here held, anatomised in such great light
That no long snow, although it fell forever
Down on the dead town, could change it here—
Alive and his because he was not theirs.

50

Portrait. Boston, 1916

If there were friends to meditate
The foolishness of his illusion,
A wiser sort may still relate
The bafflement of their intrusion;
Albeit that his kindled smile
Was innocent of wrath or guile,
His distance could consign to fate
Alike their kindness and confusion.

And yet a patient gentleness
Like a soft garment overlaid him
And turned upon the more or less
The same inbound respect that stayed him;
Until, although we stared to see
Such mingled proud humility,
We knew enough to still confess
We could not know all that had made him.

We'd stay awhile and watch him smoke
In his long-fingered concentration,
And when sometimes his humor broke
He sucked his cheeks for celebration
And twinkled with a ponderous
Gay thoughtfulness that came to us
Across an earnest league which spoke
At once of privilege and privation.

And if the scornful few had learned
But lesser ways than ours of knowing

The meaning of the flame that burned
And had not even for him foreshowing,
At least we saw within the wise
Compassion of his foreign eyes
The light that richened, unreturned,
The beggared and the unbestowing.

New Hampshire Summer, 1926

Again the seasonal return—retreat—the studied dying
Out of his time that he might see its face behind him—
Clearer for being there. What snows had fallen and gone?
What winters slowly starved while he stared them down and
    walked
Among the towers that thickened and grew taller, like dumb blind
    giants.
New York—the whiskey and the symphonies; the friends, the
    plays,
The news of triumph: behind him now; the spring
Spread on the morning sea in front of Boston—climbed the bricks
In waves of ancient gold
              that turned to summer in New Hampshire.

Could granite burn? Was there some hidden fire of the sun
Locked in the rough rock? Some closed and secret flame
Humming like a heart deep in the stone? and his to hear
Slowly, and over and over, in this large peace.

                        Peace—peace,
And the work not done. The calm and ageless trees, the blunt
Unchanged Monadnock like his shadow on the sky,
Larger with late afternoon; waiting; and then it came again—

The passionate fire flailing swift and falling
With enormous grief and tenderness that sang
Like a thousand wings flying altogether inland
To sing how love came in a seething song and consumed
All to immaculate nothing, till only the crying echo
Sounded upon the still and luminous air.

                                        Peace,
And the gaunt, tired triumph. Where is he going, this man
Among the trees? October raises a great dust and the sun
Leans long across it, the glimmering spokes of light
Slanting the woodland road through which he walks
Wrapped in a far-off meditative stoop, tall and alone.

The autumnal murmuring of the dusk dims and goes out.

New York Hospital, 1935

All his golden words are spent
And after that no man alone,
Stretched on his crumbling bed, could own
The vigilance of their intent;
He heard them then, and all they meant
Furled round his head to wings of stone.

His hands no counterfeit could buy,
The swift brain's unsurrendered flight,
The eyes' assurance of their sight—
Blazed on the body that could die:
Flesh, as it faded, gradually
Itself became created light.

Yet breathing, almost separate
From breath and insubstantial
As his thin shadow on the wall,
He waited like one told to wait
While from uncoiling night the late
And last long hours began to fall:

—Then suddenly turned his head and heard
One final golden word.

The Voices

Then in the dark all but the face was gone;
The face, luminous, hardened to staring stone.
There was no voice at all. Then gradually
The room filled with voices. They were all one.
They were all like light. They kept speaking on.
They were music and light together. They were sad
And laughing together. The face was no longer alone.
We were no longer alone. The voices kept on.

THE SWORD ON THE TABLE (1942)

History is dates, a flung sword on a table,
. . . a brave head in the dirt.
                                —Donagh MacDonagh

The Sword on the Table

What Say You, Prisoner: Will You Be Tried
   by That Juror or Not?

                              (April 30-May 6 1844)
                    Voices at the Trial:
"Have I no right to show the intent in which I acted?"

"The Court understands that the prisoner, Thomas Dorr,
Now desires to show that he was no usurper:
Taker of arms against his lawful State, but not a traitor.
Wilful seizer of governorship, but not a traitor.
Wrecker of peace and property and society, but—
So long as in his wisdom he thought this wise—no traitor.
So any John Smith might steal his neighbor's pig,
Then being haled to court cry 'Yes, I stole it;
I admit the thievery, gentlemen, but let me show you
I felt it my inherent right!'—and think to acquit himself.
This is worse than folly—it is legal folly
As the accused should know."

                         "When we gathered with Dorr at
                                Acote's Hill
To defend the people's rights, few of the people came."

"As counsel for the State, I charge the prisoner
With the crime of levying war against the State. This Court
Properly holds by law this crime is treason."

                                        "The night
Was very foggy. Couldn't tell the Arsenal from a tree.
When I met Dispeau marching off his men
I said 'Dispeau, what the devil are you doing?'
'There's danger here,' he said. I said, 'My God,

How the hell do you go into war and not into danger?'
He went off and I went in search of Dorr."

"All that was done was in the people's will. This Court
Cries treason.—My client is a Rhode Island man."

"Only a week before this trial commenced
Laban Coggeshall said on Thames Street here in Newport
He hoped Dorr hanged for his crimes."

                                        "Juror dismissed."

"Dorr's own brother manned a gun against him."

"As counsel for the State, I would ask the jurors
Two questions besides the usual questions:
'Did you vote for Thomas Dorr for governor
Under the so-called People's Constitution
At the so-called election two years ago?' And
'Do you believe the prisoner was governor
And authorised to act as governor
In May and June that year?'"

                           "Objection! Your Honor,
Justice need not discover party sentiment.
The State would beg the whole trial with those questions."

"Objection sustained."

                           "And is it not sufficient
That by a law made specially to harm him
My client must be tried in another—unfriendly—county
Than that in which his alleged crimes were committed,
Before a court which has no jurisdiction?"

"That is a question of law; the Court will decide."

58

"We hold also that the Algerine Acts
Passed to punish all who banded together
To alter an outmoded, privileged government
That had its alleged authority from King Charles' Charter,
None whatsoever from the Revolution,
Destroy common law and are not in fact the law."

"That is a question of law; the Court will decide."

"We hold also that treason cannot be done
Against a State; that Thomas Dorr is charged
With a crime impossible save against his country."

"That is a question of law; the Court will decide."

"I wish the record of this trial to show
That Your Honor, as Chief Justice of the State,
Publicly opposed the people's right of vote;
Declared the citizen's unhesitant duty
To rulership by the propertied class alone."

"The Court reminds Mr. Turner he may be barred
Further from this room for contempt of the Court."

"Thomas Dorr as governor of this State
Acted with justice and consistency
Under a rightful constitution, rightfully
Chosen by a majority of the people.
He took arms only to establish that."

"That is a question of law and a question of fact.
The Court will decide the law; as for the fact
Evidence toward it here would be irrelevant."

"My name is Dutee J. Pearce. I do not know
If on the day of the prisoner's inauguration

He favored seizing the State House. I think he did.
I have said since that but for me and my friends
Governor Dorr and his more ardent partisans
Would have forced the public property."

"That is correct; Mr. Dorr was overruled—
A most fortunate circumstance, I believe."

"Will the witness please confine himself to fact.
Confine himself to fact . . . confine to fact . . . confine fact." . . .

"All that I said was that Mr. Dorr
Seemed to me an uncommon stubborn man.
I heard him speak that day in Providence.
He drew his sword and flashed it in the sun
And his whole mob roared like infernal fiends
When he shouted out that for the people's rights
He'd see it buried to the hilt in gore."

"I was that day in the prisoner's barouche.
Mr. Dorr said only that the sword
Had honorably served an honorable fighter
Who died in Florida; he charged himself
The sword be not dishonored in his hands."

"It was but a good, hearty, honest cheer;
I stood nearby."

                    "They yelled like demons,
And when he screamed for blood Dorr looked a demon."

"Now you, Darius Hall, were among the citizens
Armed and gathered at Acote's Hill?"

                              "I was."

"That was late June—about four weeks or so
After the attempt on the Arsenal, and seven
After the prisoner's alleged inauguration?"

"I don't know that. I know only what I see.
I was not at any inaugural or arsenal."

"You are a small farmer?"

                    "I am."

                              "What
Did you suppose a band of armed men gathered for
Just inside the border of the State
Led by a man who claimed to be the governor?"

"I do not know what the armed men were there for."

"You had heard an alleged legislature might meet?"

"I doubt they were all members of the Legislature.
There were cannon there. They pointed various ways.
I saw some things that would go into cannon
With a little help. On Sunday there were rumors
That troops belonging to the State were coming—
Under slow progress. I heard a man called Dorr
Address the people. I don't know his intentions
Because I didn't interrupt to ask him.
I wasn't under anyone's control.
I considered myself a nation to myself;
Came and went as I pleased; left Sunday evening.
I believe I had some corn to hoe."

                    "Richard Knight?"

"Yes. I was held by ruffians at Acote's Hill,
Accused of being a spy from Providence.
I heard the men say they would take the State.
Carter shook a bag of shot in my face. He said
'These are the pills for you damned Algerines.' "

"I am Hiram Chappell. I thought that Acote's Hill
Was boys' play, and the cause foolish and lost.
With Dorr's men at the Arsenal attack
I plugged the cannon so they would not fire."

"Dispeau told me that when he was seized and jailed
Chappell was with him and told him at the time
He had lied to the State's men about plugging cannon."

"The night was very foggy, but I stood near the accused.
Dorr put the torch to the guns. Both flashed in the pan.
He said 'I am betrayed!' "

                    "I stood near the accused.
Dorr could not have fired the guns without my seeing it.
I do not know who fired. It was not Dorr.
As for plugging—the Almighty plugged them.
Fog damped the powder.'

                    "Gentlemen of the jury,
The Court holds it a duty to remind you
That though the accused acted as governor,
Even indeed believed in that delusion,
Which his defense admits—insists upon—
That would in no way take off his legal guilt.
The question before you is a simple question:
If by testimony of two or more
Or by confession in the open court
You find a military demonstration

Was made by the accused at Providence
Against the Arsenal; or if you find
He commanded an armed force at Acote's Hill
With the intent to overturn the State
Then it is your duty to find him guilty
For punishment with life imprisonment.
If the accused engaged in levy of war
He is by that one fact a proven traitor.
The Court has done its duty; go you to yours."

Night of the Arsenal

                                                    [May 17 1842]
                        Walter S. Burges:
I wish they'd stop tolling those bells downtown
As if the day of judgment had come at last
And come as a night of black fog, come as a hell
Sodden and cold and dripping on the shutters
And whining like the devil in the harbor.
I wish the night were over and a nightmare
To wake from and be glad it hadn't been—
The men on every corner, women at windows,
Rumors of burning the city, the guns stacked;
Now night, thick with this fog, and the armed men
Haunting the alleys

                        This is an ugly silence.
Fog's got the last torch; I can't hear them now.
Dorr must be halfway there—he and his army,
His ragamuffin cohorts; and their leader
As much a major-general as my dog.
The man's my friend, and may be dead by morning.

He knows that or he'd not have made me come
To Burrington Anthony's house—how that's like him:
To pause on the eve of civil war, and order
Legal and private papers properly
And put them in safe hands. He knows
He may be dead by morning, but he knows
He is the Governor; and he is right. Only
I wish he hadn't let it come to this.
We were winning, and were winning all the while,
But now he's raised a sword for victory
I fear he'll cut his victory to death.
There may be times that have a need of swords
And call them up like thunder and the flash,
But they come rarer than men think they come.

We had one once. The pity of it is
This little State kept fast its ancient chains.
Just so we did—let the other twelve
Write their new constitutions while we went
Hardening in the mold of King Charles' Charter,
And with our fresh-found freedom took the vote
And put it in the hands of property:
Let us be ruled by men who own the land,
By their sons, heirs, inheritors; and let us
Suffer them to legislate our lives,
Appoint our courts, and leave them the decision
Whether this be unalterable law,
—So we said and lived, and any voice
Lifted against this lying democracy
Got the chill frown of self-sufficient power.
Until Dorr's voice like an insistent ax
Cut through the iron ice, and there it was—
The clear water of freedom in the sun.
Or was it iron ice? or a sham look
Of dead light hardened on a mass of slush?

Something went wrong: was it ax or ice
Was stronger than we thought it? And now—now
All of us are split: two governors,
Two legislatures, each by separate vote,
Landholders with their Charter government,
The propertyless suddenly owning one
Along with a few class traitors like myself
And Thomas Wilson Dorr; and each of them
Crying to the President's deaf ears,
Threatening each other's threats, and now
The ax becomes a sword to meet a sword
In a hell-black fog. Or will it so?
Few as they are who march with Dorr tonight
It's likely they'll be fewer in the morning,
And even if they don't die at his side
It's likely they'll be quitting at his back.
We haven't the real temper for this storm,
And jails and fines will dampen what we have
Even if cannon do not. Poor Tom Dorr!
I wish I knew where it was right went wrong.

I've seen it twice today. Early this morning
Those cousins, kin, associates of mine—
But thinking otherwise than I, of course—
Wrangled with fear and anger in their eyes
Up and down the Town Hall corridors,
The men of means ready for compromise,
Their sons hot, unwilling. But the fear
Was there, and the readiness at last
To give, as rich men will, whatever they must
To keep their own cowardly consciences;
Or rather in the last extremity
To buy at forced sale their own peace of heart.
I told Dorr, and got no more for my pains
Than I had gotten from our enemies.

Each must be right and damn the consequence—
And something has gone wrong. I saw it there,
I saw it here again by candlelight
While Dorr and his militia—leaders all!—
Argued whether to march or not to march,
To seize the Arsenal and reveal in force
The two weeks' government by people's vote
Ringed by rightful cannon and supreme,
Or not to march against an Arsenal
Bulging with State militia already strengthened
By men who helped elect him governor
But will not follow further in this breach.
Shelley and I dissuaded him—or tried to;
Even Carter said that though the men should march
Dorr had best stay here. But go he must
With—was it ninety men that Dispeau had
Armed, most of them, with "something or other"?
"Something or other"! and the whole house banging
Till the candles rocked to boots and argument
As though a bullies' school had been let loose
And shouting "There'll be no boys' play tonight!"
God help us all, I wish it were not this.

What a bull head my friend has grown himself
That he'll go charging into fiery brush
Because he can't bear red and doesn't care
Whether it's burning so he proves it's red
Even if it scorches him.

                    And yet—yet
He isn't really wrong. Ah, Tom—arrayed
In frock coat and white belt for battle
And suddenly focusing his legal brilliance
Upon the problem of a gun: which end?
I would laugh if I weren't afraid of tears.

Fog on a city of the dead, and one bell
Tolling on as if the wind rocked it,
Night like a wall built against these windows,
Candlelight on the black glass like terror
Swaying weak, alone, with little time.
Somewhere something began to go wrong,
Now it is wrong, and now it is late.
Now it is late and dark. It is too late.

Fortnight ago at Dorr's inaugural
I thought the trick was turned, the thing done.
Governor King and his crowd in Newport,
An old government not yet renewed
Save by a ballot well discredited,
And Dorr and his in Providence by choice
Definite and irrevocably made
By vote of all the people of the State—
A clear majority of adult men
I thought we'd done it—fairly, honestly,
Legitimately as we could work it out
In the face of an entrenched and bitter class
That saw its power challenged, overthrown,
Railed and spat threats yet took no step
Even to work the foul Algerine law
Set up to save a dying dynasty
By persecuting all who did it in.
And there was Dorr marching from Hoyle's Tavern,
From Christian Hill downtown to the Foundry,
A thicket of swords, canes, muskets, guns around him,
But hundreds unarmed and the sun of May
Free and easy. And six streets from there
There was the State House and its janitor—
Records, trappings, the stage itself vacant.
Should those who marched tonight have marched then?
We'd have been done with marching. None who saw

The oaths taken, heard the inaugural,
Watched the new legislature quickly affirm
A constitution, an American law,
Could for a moment doubt the thing was done.
And what could King and his decrepit crew
Have made of all their letters to the White House
Their cries of insurrection and rebellion
If de facto and de jure, Dorr
Sat in the State House with his votes behind him,
Accredited militia all around him
And the machinery of State before him?

What have we got instead? King in his chair
—Dorr's chair—and his owners' government
All seated with a quite legitimate look.
More letters to the White House, Fort Adams
Doubled in garrison, and General Scott's
Daily report; and now Dorr in the trap,
Rushing to Washington, finding New York friends,
Returning with a sword and a threatening speech,
And now beyond the cure of compromise
This bitter black night that I wish undone.

When this fog lifts and also lifts the night
What there will be to see will not be good
To look at, will not be fair to live with;
As though by premonition of a doom
That midnight bell tolls prophecy of dark
That will not lift with night or fog or any
Power now all powers have darkness in them,
And what rose bright to live lies stained with death.

I don't know why I wish the day would come.

Night in the Arsenal

The Arsenal commanded a plain west of the city.
50 x 60 feet, two stories, and chip stone walls.
The walls were 28 inches thick at the base and tapered
To 18 at the top; and there were 28 windows, 2 doors.
Below and above, at every window, the State's men
Leveled their muskets into a sea of fog
And were as baffled as blind men at windows
Of a sunken city on the ocean's floor.
They might have been dead sentries of an Atlantis fort
Damned to some after-living life on guard
To hold an inundated, swaying ruin,
Sure that within the tides that rocked above them
A final, living enemy approached.

                              Inside,
Civilization, sane and recognizable:
200 men in arms; grape, round and canister shot,
Ball cartridges in piles; 5 six-pound cannon:
One each side; one center; one at each iron door.
Candle and lamp light pitched in a damp draught,
A door clanged and Colonel Leonard Blodget,
In command, pistol in hand, stamped in.

"Nothing to do but sit tight," Blodget said.

"See anything?"

          "I've been lying on the ground—
Until I thought my belly'd freeze in the damp.

I could hear them talking but I couldn't see them.
Once the mist lifted a little—I saw their cannon.
Brass gleamed in torch light."

"How many?"

"Five or six, I guess. That is what they took
This afternoon at the Artillery building.
Been lugging them all around town ever since."

"You don't think Tom Dorr can fire a cannon!"

"No, but he may have somebody who can.
No telling how many thugs he's rounded up
To fight his little war."

"Do you think they'll fight?"

"Ah, Governor King! We're honored, sir; but may I say
You'd better not be here. Fog or no fog, and
Dorr or no Dorr, we may get cannon shot
Crashing upon us."

"Let them have it first!"

"Unless the weather changes, or they fire,
We can't be accurate as to where they are.
And after all we have a defensive position
Against a threat which still remains a threat."

"I'd say their seizure of the Artillery cannon
Began the offensive, Blodget, hours ago—
You know they held up Colonel Bennett's men.
Why, they began to force the place with bayonets
Till Bennett gave the guns up. Man named Reed

Seemed to be in charge. He said he acted
On orders from 'Governor Dorr'—'Governor Dorr'!
If you ask me, Colonel Blodget, Tom Dorr's mad
And should be shot down like a dangerous dog!"

"No doubt, sir. Yet Dorr may be gesturing once
To satisfy the rabid in his camp.
Some of my men early this evening mingled
With Dorr's crowd over at Anthony's house
And they think—let's sit here on these kegs,
If you please, Governor.'

                    The thud of boots
Paced in a restless prison march above them,
And on the lower floor men sat about,
All save the primed and silent at the windows.
Even their voices made a humming stillness
Equal and level in the dim, smoky air.
In the actual silences a dull bell
Tolled as if far and muffled in the city,
But none spoke of it nor seemed to listen.
Some were not uniformed, and most who were
Looked equally innocent of property,
But they were moved as men are by the fear
Of change, when faced with powers that challenge power
That after all is certain and requires
Only a man's allegiance to respond
That his proportionate security
Rests on Things That Are; and they were there,
The job-holders and fathers, with their courage
That there should be no courage toward the Law,
And some of those who were the Law, or their
Sons, were also there with their sincerity
Unquestionable, being inherited.

"They were maybe twenty or thirty yards away,"
Edward Hazard said. "Smith and I lay down
Near Blodget, and we could hear them yelling,
Telling one another to pull the drag-ropes;
And we could hear the ropes slap and the cannon
Rolling as though being readied in position.
They have the guns all right, and probably loaded,
According to what Whipple saw at Anthony's."

"Sure, they've got stuff to fire," Whipple said.
"I saw Dorr giving money to a man
And heard Dorr order him to buy powder.
The man went off. That was early evening."

"If they'd clapped Dorr in jail two weeks ago
We'd all be done with this."

                              "I understand
Sheriff Roger Williams Potter's pocket
Has warmed a warrant since the fourth of May."

"That's true," said an officer named Ives.
"Potter himself told me this very morning.
I can't make him out. 'Why don't you nab Dorr?'
I asked him in the Square. And Potter said
Well, he'd been looking. 'Looking?' I said
'Yes,' he said, damp as a clam. He said
He'd seen Dorr the day that Dorr returned,
But there was our self-appointed 'governor'
In his barouche surrounded by armed men.
'Couldn't arrest him then, Mr. Ives,' says Potter.
'Maybe you were frightened by that sword he waved,'
I said to Potter. 'Oh, no, sir,' says he,
Giving me that blank, fat stare he has

I don't fathom him. All the reason he had
Was that he couldn't find Dorr: been looking for him
Around the streets, mind you."

                              "Yet it's true
Nobody knows where Dorr is hanging out."

"Certainly, but when I inquired of Potter
If he'd gone to Burrington Anthony's,
He said he didn't apply there; said he'd got it
From General Carrington that Dorr might be
At the *Herald* office or at the *Express.*
Potter's either a dummy or a scoundrel."

"Dorr alone might have scared him," Whipple said.
"When he reappeared here yesterday
I never saw him look so bad. He looked
Haggard and worn, his face all smooched with dust,
His beard ragged and his eyes blazing.'

"Say, where's Dorr?"

                    "Where's Dorr! For God's sake,
Out there in the soup. Where'd you think?"

"No, I mean his brother, Sullivan."

"Here I am." A young, thick-legged man
Came into the circle by the lamp.
His State militia uniform looked new,
The set of his face looked older than his face.
"I've just been relieved at the south window."
He sat on the floor, his musket across his thighs.
The sound of the bell tolled suddenly loud

Then rocked away again. "It's all right," he said,
"Go on saying whatever you were saying.
You can see, can't you, which side I'm on?"

"We know," said Ives, "where you stand, Sullivan.
Too damned bad all this had to be."

"Yes; he's surrounded now by such rabble
As you would think no gentleman would spit upon,
Let alone choose for cronies," Sullivan said.
"If Tom wants a genuine picture of his cause,
Why don't he take a look at those around him,
The malcontents, ex-jail-tenants, the mob.
He's heard them and they make so loud a noise
He thinks the people speak. A brother's reasons,
A father's and a mother's tears are nothing
Under that blast of foul-breathed, public shouting.

"I heard Smith say no one knows where Tom lives.
That's right. He's left my father's house and left
My mother's heart broken.—Why, we all know
If what Tom wanted was to be Governor
There was nothing in his way. He's smart—smart as any
Man in the State: has held responsible office,
Been brilliant in the courts, had the respect
Of everyone who counted; he could have risen
Easily to the governorship and—who knows?—
Far beyond it maybe. But he got
This fool idea to upset everything,
And once he's got an idea, hell itself
Won't blast him off it. He was always that way:
Stubborn and wilful."

                    "The way I look at it,"
Said Stephen Crawford: "Your brother may have had

The best intentions in the world. Know how it is.
Then a few radicals and one or two
Unscrupulous traitors like that Walter Burges
Who've got no responsible feeling toward the way
They've been brought up, or toward their own position,
—I don't say Tom was really one of them—
Talked him into thinking all Rhode Island
Was ready to go anarchist; and then that vote,
Stuffed though it was, made it all seem legal."

"My brother wouldn't condone a dirty vote!"

"O, probably he wouldn't, Sullivan.
But he can be deceived enough, can't he?
We all know that that vote couldn't be honest.
There aren't that many workingmen deluded
Into defying a government that guards them,
Protects their rights, work, families and freedom.
What workingman do you know who aspires
To take on responsibilities of State?
Why, they're not trained or educated for it,
They get a square deal and they're satisfied
—All but a noisy few."

                          "You needn't argue,"
Sullivan Dorr said, staring at the lamp.
"I've shown clearly enough that I agree—
Or don't you think so?" and he glared at Crawford.
"If it's plain words you want—plainer than yours—
Then you may have whatever satisfaction
You may have in hearing Tom's brother say
That Tom is ruthless, vain, ambitious,
Heartless and irresponsible, and puts
The working out of all of his delusions

Above the peace of his own State and family,
Which comes about to the same thing—"

                                    They all
And all the others in the room looked up,
Sprang to their feet, guns handy. And there was
A second loud rap on the iron door.
Before anyone had made a move, the sentry
Entered and slammed the heavy door behind him.

"There's a man here with a flag of truce!"

Colonel Blodget said nothing. With pistol drawn,
He went to the door and held it open: all
Could see in a mist of torch light and blown fog
A more or less anonymous man alone.

"Are you Colonel Blodget?"

                    "Yes, I am."

"I demand the surrender of this Arsenal."

"By what authority?"

                    "By the command
Of Colonel Wheeler and of Governor Dorr."

"I have no knowledge of any Colonel Wheeler
Nor any Governor Dorr."

                    The torch hissed
In the wet night; and for a tolled moment all—
Those in, those out unseen,—seemed to wait.

Night Outside the Arsenal

[May 18 1842]

Carter stood at Governor Dorr's left, Kendall at his right—
Just as they had marched to the plain earlier
When they were still more than misty shadows
To know each other by. Colonel Wheeler turned
Away from the Governor and said "Carter,
You are to take a flag of truce to the Arsenal.
Demand its surrender."

    "What shall I say?"

"Just say that we will blow them all to hell."

"That's not a civil message."

     "Well, write your own."

Carter took a torch and by its light
Fastened a handkerchief to his musket-barrel,
Then moved off slowly. They could see
His torch as a thin glow only a little way. . . .

"I shall not surrender the Arsenal," said Blodget,
Squinting against the torch light by the door.

"We have a large force and we shall take it."

"Then come and take it." . . .

Wheeler whispered
As soon as Carter found him, "What did he say?"

"What the hell do you think he said? He said
That he'd defend it."

He saw Wheeler turn away
Three steps, and he had vanished. To his right
Carter heard sounds as of many men
Scuffling a careful way together. "Hello!"
He shouted. Captain Dispeau emerged
Suddenly before him. "What are you doing, Dispeau?"

"Marching off my men. There's danger here."

"Danger! How the devil do you go to war
And not get into danger?" But Dispeau
Said nothing and disappeared in fog again.
Carter heard a man say "Come along.
The whole thing's a fizzle and you know it";
And heard the company shuffling slowly off.

Then there was Kendall. "It looks bad, Carter—
As much of it as you can see in this pitch.
But I'm afraid that if we had sudden starlight
It might look worse. Poor Tom's feeling his way
From one shadow to another—there aren't many—
Trying to rally such men as are left.
Of the two hundred and thirty who came along
I doubt if there are more than thirty here."

"See if you can find Dorr," Carter said,
"And ask what's to be done. Tell him for me
It might be just as well to sound retreat
And gather our forces for a better chance.
If he gives up now it needn't be for keeps.

We've still four kegs of powder and five cannon,
Plenty of bullets and more where they came from."

—But Kendall had already gone and soon,
Surprisingly, was there again. "Carter?—
The men are badly scattered. There's a handful
Still with Dorr. He says you take command."

"He isn't going to fire on them now!"

"Yes. He insists.

    "Good God, Kendall,
Wheeler had better be right, after all.
Either we blow the Arsenal to hell
Or there'll be massacre if we misfire!"

Around them in the dark nobody moved.
No sound came from the Arsenal, which still
Lay as lost before them as though nothing
Lived in the night but their few unreal ghosts.
Dorr's white cross-belt on his stolid bulk
Took the glare of torch light now and then;
His face was darkened under his leather cap,
His unmilitary body a frock-coated
Girthy shadow, quiet as a statue and like stone.

Carter ordered two cannon aimed, unlimbered.
Hathaway tended right gun, Andrews the left,
Their faces hot and strained when the light caught them.

"Prime right piece!"

   "Yes, sir."

    "Touch it off!"

Fire hissed and flashed in the pan. Nothing.
Night again and with a weightier silence
Because no bells were sounding any more.
Carter said, "Go ahead, Andrews." The left cannon
Hissed and flashed, and Carter ran toward it,
Tried the priming wire. It would not go down.
"This powder's rotten with fog. It's turned cement.
Hathaway, are you ready once again?'

                            "Yes, sir."

But before Carter spoke a man leaped forward
Swinging his torch toward the right gun. It flashed
Dead again. "This is betrayal," he said
From the sudden darkness of his blown-out light.

Who Is the Prisoner at the Bar?

                                    [May 6 1844]
            Thomas W. Dorr:
Have I no right to show the intent in which I acted?
I face you through force of law especially enacted
To levy upon me and those who were with me harsh punishment.
This court, which would sentence me to life imprisonment
For treasonous acts, knows what stress the law lays upon intent.
On score of motives, I esteem my testimony important.

Though I have been an exile, I have been a Rhode Island man
All my life; and what in the course of duty I have done
I have done it as the people's will—and if it is not
Permitted me to show this, I may still hope this is not forgot.
I have heard it said here in a not unfriendly voice

That a man is a nation unto himself and acts in that choice.
This is not so: the people are the entire people—none
Whether in property or penury can act above them and alone.
The people are a pyramid, and base to top stand as one stone.

You have heard that on the night of attack upon the Arsenal
I fired the cannon that flashed and I cried out "Betrayal!"
This is not so. I gave the order to attack and fire.
I waved no torch, applied no match. Had I the desire
So to have done, I had the right; I did not choose to use it.
With elected power yet I would not knowingly abuse it
As a military amateur. At the house of Burrington Anthony
I declared that the people's party was welcome to the whole of me,
Since we must march against the Arsenal, then I
Should not be found in the rear; and so also at Acote's Hill
The following month, I again led the military as in the people's
    will.
This is all that this Court asks you to know or care—
That there occurred levies of war and that I was there.
This alone is said to be criminal.—Well, then, I was there.

Despite disaster, despite those forced excursions and alarums,
The rights of a case are not taken away by a failure of arms.
We did so fail and yet nothing is altered from what was made
Because it was made by the people's vote, and none afraid,
Or loath to act, or indifferent, could abandon it by their deeds,
And it is alive now with a valid blood that bleeds
Out of the wounds of justice given here; also I would contend
It cannot be lost, though it were surrendered by every friend.
What the people do they can undo, and what they undo they
Can make new again but always, only in their sovereign way.

On the morning after the Arsenal attack, many had withdrawn
As from a hopeless cause; and certain State officers, I was shown,
Had overnight resigned; and again at Acote's Hill too few

Rallied to sustain their rights as men will fail to do—
As men will falter in the face of such tyrannous laws
As those with which the propertied class fought the people's
    cause—
Fines levied, men jailed, trials out of county where the "crime"
    occurred,
Life in chains for an alleged treasonable act and word—
All done with a potentate's, a dictator's revenge
On a people who dared fling before his chariot their challenge.

I speak to you, gentlemen, before the highest judge of this State
And he has said that the true people are the people corporate,
That they are the sovereign people, the landed folk; that the rest
Unhesitatingly demean themselves in the interest
Of responsible government. But I say that this is not
The life for which in '42 or in '76 we and our fathers fought.
This country has no plan to light the few and damn the lot.
There are expediencies that are fair sometimes—in love and war.
I left the State on May 18th, '42, and for
A reasonable reason, I believe. I was the elected Governor,
The first this State as a whole people had, and therefore
Had certain duties to perform, and they were better done
Outside the walls of a prison than undone within one.
The privileged people whom the people had opposed
Went rampant in retaliation and with a force supposed
As legal as large; and I had none or little—I had
Only my office, a wrecked Assembly—I knew not how bad—
Adjourned, pledged to meet on the first, July.
Late in June I returned to the State from Killingly
And with me were Michael Walsh and his New York men;
The Spartans, they were called. At Chepachet I came again
Because word had reached me that at last a sufficient force
Had mustered to protect the government in its course;
There at Acote's Hill I found perhaps two hundred;

Some left, a few more came—none was hindered.
A larger hill commanded Acote's; our breastworks there
Were pathetic brush and dirt; there were rumors of Charter
Troops along the way from Providence—two thousand or more.
They did not come until they heard there would be no war,
Then came to seize disarmed, disbanded men
To make a mock parade as victors. As to that, when
They did come, my followers weren't much less disarmed than
    they had been.
And as to the strangers with me, I had always said
That if the alleged governor, Mr. King, had succeeded
In bringing Federal troops into this State,
Our volunteers from anywhere should be ready with equal right.
Myself, I came again with an apparent hope—
Not to make war but to find our cause in all its scope
Readied at last, defended and maintained
And all we had gained at long last surely gained.

This hope I abandoned soon enough. At Acote's Hill
Farmers, mechanics, the rough-handed men of will,
Men—most of them—of good will, had gathered round.
They'd not enough provision, not enough lead to pound
Fifteen minutes of cannon fire in all.
Yet that was not our end. Saturday, Sunday, till nightfall
Monday I waited. Already there were fewer and all
The rest, the rumored rest, had not come; I'd heard a claim
Six hundred would come from Providence, and thirty came;
Fifteen hundred from all the State—but almost none,
And that was our end and our single consideration.
For whatever reasons, we could no longer contend
A majority were with us and I gave the order to disband.
I had had a friend who had advised me: that friend
Headed the State's forces against us; and I heard
How the State's forces—but also the official word

Of a new constitution, though of course none was needed—
Had taken all but the few who had not succeeded
In throwing down what we had truly sought and made.

They told me Walsh swore and struck his sword in the sand.

There are times, occasions, luck and lack of it
And rarely a man given both the wisdom and the wit
To bring a dream alive, to take what splendor rises
From men themselves, to make them see, their eyes his,
And build the desired state into the actual.
One man can see much, be helped, yet not see all.
"There is a tide . . . which taken at the flood—" you know it,
And had we been borne on to fortune through it,
This would be a happier and a freer State for us;
And for that, few indeed could have sworn other purpose.
Some triumph—true—has been accomplished in the wake
Of our attainments and misfortunes; for the sake
Of quieting fearful consciences, new laws were made
—They were not needed, and the cause of their engendering was
    sad.
Nor are some older, vicious laws dead: by them, I am here.

Gentlemen, it is important to me that I make all things clear
That appertain to things I did or did not do.
What spots the books before our time every one of you
Knows and recalls, and how year following year
Petitioners who held the democratic causes true and dear
Were all but spat upon by power held, entrenched.
What we did desperately when we wrenched
That power from the few that all might rightfully bear it
We did because we had to or else never share it.
Privilege and duty are so joined and interwoven
None but the greedy grasp it all, and none but the sloven
Stands idly at such sight of greed. But there are times,

There are occasions, luck, ill-luck; and it may be our crimes
As often are the things we do not do as those we do.
You have heard here that on my inaugural day
I did desire to march into the State House—the way
Was clear, the vote commanded it. And that is so.
Overruled by friends who advised against and would not follow
I did not pursue what seemed the proper course.
After that day of victory all our cause became a wild loss.
In that I failed the people, and if after that
It seems the people continually failed in what
Their better, stronger days had shown them as their path,
I am willing that it be remembered in glee or wrath
That I mis-stepped and lost them much—lost all.
When I fought on it was because I could not believe we'd fail.
Nor did we truly fail. Tricks fail from knowledge, slow but every-
        where
Always at the last; and what we did we have always, even here.

Have I no right to show what my intentions were?
I have maintained that treason against a State's
An impossible crime, since these United States
Stand as a federated one, and treason can be done to it alone.
I have maintained the Act of March—the Algerine—
"Relating to the offenses against the (so-called) Sovereign
Power of the State," voids common law and is unconstitutional.
I have maintained that if this Court, after all,
Holds that act valid, then this Court has no jurisdiction
Over alleged crimes in another county, not in this one.
I have maintained that all my acts were justified
Under a true constitution, legally ratified,
And that I swore to uphold—did swear and do still.
And fifth I have maintained that not a jot or tittle
Of evidence supports the State's charge of treason.

The State insists, first and last, that treason was done
First and last. The first four points of the defense
This Court itself decides as legal technics, will hear no evidence
On any of them. And on the treason charge the Court maintains
That evidence to convict me to a life in chains
Need only be that I was there. I am not allotted
Even the right to produce the votes that were balloted
On April 18th, 1842, and which would show
That I was Governor and honestly elected so.—No,
Nothing in this Court will be received as fair
Evidence save that armed men marched and I was there.

That is so. All that I say here now can bear
Little or nothing on what you twelve men leave to do
Since I have from the beginning spoken to you
With chains already on me—and that I had not thought
When voluntarily I came home again to clear my lot,
And with mine so many hundred afflicted more
Punished by the powers that in long truth they fought for.
Difference of opinion—yes; that I cherish. My own brother
Opposed all that so many of us held. And—here—my nearest
    friend,
Walter Burges, could not believe that we should take arms to
    defend
What we both agreed was truth. Yet my brother, were he not in
    a foreign land,
Would be here at my side in these days, like this good man—my
    right hand.

The rights a people have are those they care for—they
Must be worthy of their innate rights or they
Shall get only those that they are worth. The laws
Are not made for the few but by the many, because
Burdens of State must be distributed to be rightly borne.
These things are true and upon them we are sworn

Or we are nothing, and all the brighter promise of this land
Shadowed in a dark; and if that darkness rise and stand
Here in this hope of earth, then will it deepen elsewhere.
We must stay strong as our intentions were.
The right of freedom is the people's right. This Court decides
That in that declaration the idea of revolution hides.
And that is so. It seems to interest this Court
That the people, who are all the people, have too a last resort.
Legislatures, it is true, make laws. People make legislatures
And what they make they can unmake if they choose.

There are times, occasions, wit, ill-luck, but never a time
When the people are not sovereign. No crime
Of treason can be levied on a people in act together
Either as one or a majority—or on any man whoever
That acts as they command. This is no monarch's thing,
This country, as if in any single individual, impossible king,
The sovereign power were summed up and enthroned.
Here power is everywhere or evil, owned everywhere, loaned,
Taken again and given again: power here is republican
And in all chambers of that house our tenancy is common.
Any can be lifted up because any can be thrown down.
The law shall say to president, pauper, to any man
What he shall do or not do in the public good,
But the public shall say—at last—though late—the lawful word.

Sovereignty of light is no man's private estate,
No man's particular inheritance; but, even to those who wait
A long time in the night, the light will come, and it was with them
Even in the darkness so long as they believed it all that time
In however black and evil night; and so the world be won
Freely to the whole light; for where the people are, there is the sun.

TO MARRY STRANGERS (1945)

The Children

Here come the children like tricky leaves let loose;
There they go down the hill on a meadow wind.
We the begetters watch but cannot say whose.
They are never ours and their number seems never thinned.

They are the only foreign race, and they have
No nation and they are never a generation;
We can be lost or pre-war, free or slave,
But children and history have nothing in common.

Here they come like expectant petitioners
Hoping that we may tell them what to ask—
But there they run from unimagined answers
Save these few who stay at last and accept our mask.

But there they run with ranks all undiminished.
I hear they are the future, yet it is not so:
Whatever we have wished, since they have not wished,
They are rather present perfect but they do not know.

They do not change forever, or we should remember
Who have no knowledge but the conscious breath
Of those filled deep with the grief of being clever.
It is we that subtracted time and divided death.

Contradictions in an Ultimate Spring

I write this, Lindsay, for your later time;
In the spring of 1944, before
Invasion of the European lands,
And on the day Rome falls. I write, as one
Too old and too preoccupied to go,
To tell you what it was not to be there
But to be here where you as a small boy
Are too young even to know what we await.
Written for reading in a public place
Perhaps even after the terror has begun,
After that, my son, this is for you—
My testament of one spring but not my will.

No man wills hell, yet all inherit it
At one time or another; and in my time
All were brought up in hell because too many
Possessing fire that amiably warmed them
Did not mind how many more it burned,
Or see how fire grown wide and tall with lust
Would not leave alone even its keepers.
So this spring we make the final gesture
Out of deliberate necessity:
Fight fire with fire. The supposition is,
Ours to extinguish theirs. And it may be
If you grow up into a fairer country,
Then because of this; though maybe not;
I do not know and I cannot predict
Being one concerned only with what is real—
A poet, if your generation please.

I only know a flame marches toward Europe
To meet another there and that what matters,
Now both are loosed, is what remains after
Both of them go out, if both go out.
I know that this is not a torch we bear
Though some men say it is, as good men said
Twenty-five years ago this was the torch;
But no, this is the flag of hell itself,
This is breath of death, flame without light.
Deliverance—*lux et veritas*—may lift
Its fiery staff from this: it is not this.

Honor, dishonor marry every day
Meaning to get them honorable children.
I question this in nations or in people.
The black strain, the inheritance, continues
Since no man gelds himself; and on all sides
Truth embarrasses all champions' strength—
They tend to leave a little by the way,
Find that going easy they go farther.
Truth is not a weapon but a light;
It does not fight; it is. My only hope,
My son, is fighting men will come to it
In terrible extremity, and know it.
Alas, it shines best in the darkest hour
But in the glaze of victory seems to fade.
All men espouse more affable influence—
Make no mistake: winners and losers too—
Beget again our repetitious world,
That damned, magnificent monstrosity,
Its marvelous muscles and its hidden cancer.
If only those who pray this second morning
On which I write this verse, now overnight
Invasion has begun, would know enough
What to pray for and to whom to pray.

But that will do for that. I speak of spring
Which came this year as hesitant as ever
Yet like a virgin half-bespelled, once touched,
Opened with such passionate responses
We were ourselves half-frightened, all amazed,
And said it never was like this before.
Flowers beyond flowers over flowers
All the swift extravagance of spring
Had us drunken: desire, satiety
So mixed that we were numb and might have said
That if this were our last spring it embraced
More than we remembered of all springs
And justified the earth, mankind aside.
Maybe this is the spring you will remember
Now you are four years old, although of course
You will not know what spring you remember.

Let me put down, for you to read sometime,
You helped me plant pansies and lettuce, both,
And were most diligent and over-generous
Watering them at evening, and very proud.
This June I saw you in a field of daisies
Deep as your eyes—only your blond mop showing
Above the white and gold; and I daresay
This is the depth you will remember daisies
All your life, disturbed in June's hot smell
On shallower fields in shorter afternoons.
You liked to walk about the yard and prod
Me into naming names: peony, maple,
Poppy, iris, robin, lady-bug, tulip,
Lilac, snowball, hyacinth, bleeding-heart.
Worm you knew. And this was the spring
You came holding out buttercups to me;
I struck them from your hands and turned away
From all that shining which was partly flowers.

94

Will you forgive me, knowing that I loved you?
Will I forgive you for loving me?
Can we undo the ancestral Protestant
And in a spring that blossomed on a red wall
Acknowledge purgatory and hope for heaven?
Lives like nations break, but if for love
Is what we have to know after the battle.
This is the spring you ordered dug a foxhole,
Naming it; and I dug it for you.
Dirty and happy you lay down in it,
Above a stick you made machine-gun sounds,
That vicious riveting we did not know
Which is the new yell of your generation.
Otherwise I recognize the same
Recurrent calls of comradeship and vengeance
And think how unalterably as seasons
Children repeat the patterns of their games,
Are somehow nearer crocuses and sparrows
Than us adult. That you may go on,
Elsewhere we slay children accidentally:
Send up to God the cry of innocent blood.

Let me see your face. And I will look
And think as all men looking at their sons
Think beyond words, staring at radiance.
Generation after generation
This is what we slay—as though we had
Imagined vengeful gods, invented altars
For sacrifice, although our sons were real.
And never is the lamb produced in time;
And never is the pouring blood rewarded;
Dawn is dark as ever; if glory shone
It went out with the sons: survivors are
Those knowing how to live with dead hearts.
Unsullied April light—this radiance—

That from our loins, as surely as all else
That springs from earth, is the true child of earth,
This intention or miraculous accident:
What is it that we cannot keep? What is it
That is too natural and pure for us?
What is it we must cripple, kill, deny?
What innocence too naked to be known?

Stand in the sun and let me see your face.
You cannot stand so far away from me
But that my shadow falls upon you still.
You run across the field but calling back
Begging me to follow: if I turn
And cannot follow, in a moment you—
I know—will turn again and run to me.
By what long preservations and escapes
We have arrived here, both reluctant births;
And for what do I stand astride your morning
But to remember thus the day begins,
That there are conflagrations that are flowers
Meadow into meadow where a child
Can walk and not be harmed a little while.
Perhaps I shall not fail you more than this
Will fail you, as it must; not any more
Than I could recompense you for this hour
In which by being here you bring me back,
Reminding me, though hell burn everywhere,
This utterance, this hope, this seeming purpose
Persists; and that the resurrected life
No matter what I do shines on your face,
Even yet the will and testament of the sun.

June 5-16 1944

96

To L. B. S.

Sometimes, tired, I imagine your death:
By childish illness, reasonless accident
Stopped still forever, gone; until I loathe
Fool dramatizations of the brain—I won't,
Though I could, write them into pictures here.

My child, outlive me! Stay beyond my times
Which—how I see now—could be worse than these,
As they are worse for many who had sons.
Death I can bear for myself once, not twice.
I am out of bed at midnight to beg this.

Annual Legend

A million butterflies rose up from South America,
All together, and flew in a gold storm toward Spain:
Eastward, the annual legend, a shining amber cloud
Driven homeward as it had been and would be again
Since the conquerors searching the harder shining
Brought for the bargain a handful of wings of flame.

Balboa lies dead somewhere and Pizarro's helmet
Is a spider's kingdom; yet here was the arrogant breath
And the dangerous plume burning across the foreign air
That danced like an ancient Andalusian noon:
A blaze, it rose leaving the jungle dark and the leaves

97

Heavy with silence, and the wheeltracks folding to doom
Where majesty wandered:

A million butterflies,
Wheeling eastward from the soil where the nugget lies lost,
Turned homeward in vast diurnal fire that marched one day
Burning toward Spain; and after that, for a while,
Spread like a field of death, gold on the sea.

How Voyage Safely?

And so awoke at midnight at midsea
Deep in the shuddering ship, and knew the chill
Black waters pressing in upon my blood
That tore me out of sleep and battered my heart;

And shelved below the swaying waves could hear
Voices of stewards did not know this horror
But walked away and faded talking far
Off from my ether country and the bell of death;

And rode wide-eyed into the ocean gully
Thick with a false heat and the smell of wood
As though a house were mad and wildly strayed
From its environment and now would snap;

And carried me toward an inevitable hell
With murmurs, *This is no dream after all,*
That mounted drumming into scalding screams,
And I entangled in a sheeted sweat;

And waited for the long slide under water:
First easy, then the chandeliers and coral
Bumping together, and last the soft enmeshing
Of girders, weeds, mud, and the eyes of the dead;

And thought, Whatever made us hope to voyage
Safely: no more than bugs a moment clinging
To a thin fin once arched out of this wallow
Halfway from Europe to America.

The Starfish and the Sign

Gray water. The snow-fed sea,
Snow-blind air whisper together.
Sanded wind worries beach rubble,
Rubber shoe, frozen fish, paper.

(Inland, snow falls on hoods,
On roads and trees and roofs; snow falls
Through snow and over snow, it covers
Steeples, posts, incinerators.)

Hard starfish at my feet: the storm
Makes no white grave of winter here—
All that is dead lies naked to the air,
Sea and wind and salt reject the service.

And yes, the hidden moon moves this.
All earth freeze up—the dead planet
Will haul this useless tide over and off
And over this iron beach. TO LET. TO LET.

As for Myself

And it is after supper, and it is bright early summer early
    evening,
And under the window my father clips the high hedge on
    and on
Having mowed the lawn, and it is a grass smell cooling
At the open window over the rambler roses, and also
It is my mother shuffling the dishes out in the kitchen no less
Than it is the wind rising dark under Murphy's trees
Across the street, and a feeling of dusk and stars soon but
    not quite
And it is bright still although it is evening, and it is.

Poem

I walked through town with a dirty face and, on the whole,
More strangers spoke to me than usual.

Landescapes

(*For Waldo Kaufer's paintings*)

Here is the dried sea-floor and a
Memory of commemorative music.

This clay is grilled with the parch of
Yesterday's sun, and cracked and polished;
And lucent as velvet or metal in the—
Beyond leafless trees—starless twilight.

No print is walked here and all roses
Are dead roses, and all stones are covered.
Who knows if these are shore rocks or mountains
Now that the sky has died and come down?

Yet here is the cast leaf, red and bitter,
Rusted and stained, and another brown and surrendered.

Only an old man and two graven torsos
Stare toward these canyons, these craters, this
Drained and chilling hour that in silence
Pushes forth the heads of dolls inverted.

Still. Still. Windless earth, its last gully
Darkening, the clay returned to clay and
Dust resuming dust, and all that was merry
Curled in a crotch: the seahorse's delicate skeleton.

Stiff leaves . . . gray rose . . . embalmed faces
Of the dolls . . . in the light's evaporation
Lost here from love. There is no statement.

Headless dream of a remembered future.

To All Objectivists

Beyond O'Ryan's bar in the dirty river
A swimming rat climbed supple to the piles,
Had half an empty orange in its teeth.

At the rail above I watched it first as color,
Presently thought of it as rat and rind,
Then played upon the line of rat and me.

Now you ask, which was it of the three?

It had no knowledge of its orange-silver,
Nor differentiation, food from swill;
No reckoning of Scott in its beliefs.

Now you say, then it was none of these?

Rather I think that it was all together
Because I watched it carefully awhile
And made it whole by my necessity:

As I exist because you have imagined me.

Go Little, My Tragedy

I

My hand that never yet has touched the dead
And that the sun has never quite made warm,
Reaches, closes on itself, suspended
Halfway between the fire and the worm;
Halfway between my body and the world
It moves among the living, perilous
That it be known too closely or be held
Too nearly and its knuckle cold be lost;
It has the winter sickness of my time
Which does not die and yet is not alive

More than a dreamer wishing in a dream
He will not take back what he will not give,
Who sweats to wake at last and understand
If this be his, or all men's, or God's hand.

II

When I was twenty and a man of promise,
Innocent of time, at ease with it,
Nowhere by moonlight, I remember this
Friend of mine who said—he was explicit—
I'd do my best work in the next ten years.
Even though he spoke—of course I knew—
Less of my than his expected cheers,
Designing epics when my rhymes were through.
Thirty wakes me—and what have I done?
Shelley and Keats are younger now than I,
Chatterton's a child sure of the sun,
Only Yeats and Hardy comfort me:
These days, a river darkening and slow—
The nights a dream of it fired in the snow.

III

Memory of young and living nakedness:
O when I was twenty and in love,
Doped by day and half the night sleepless,
Doomed and saved and dazed and waked by love:
And, of course, moneyless for love and houseless,
Sure that earlier passions had not been love,
Swept back and forth from tenderness to madness
To eat and breathe and think my love, my love—
Not to possess her each day: not to possess
Her surety and fidelity as proved,
And every hour I could not see her, guess

A hundred men might see her and be moved.
At thirty, I wonder for a moment where
She is, how gold is all that golden hair.

IV

The candle dripping makes a breast of wax
Translucent, perilous in its own light;
Watching, at once I dread it may relax
But slowly it fills solid and is white;
So at the center of the circling night
This public staff performs a miracle,
Beneath the hot engender of my sight
Thus moves a little and becomes a girl.
Suddenly I am emptied of my strength;
Memory of young and living nakedness
Flares in my brain, hands, knees, my length
All voltaged with a wild paralysis;
O that that makes me larger than I was
And can diminish me in its same cause!

V

The light of the city has murdered the light of the moon.
The moon will spin no moths, nor lift our eyes.
So much filament flares out of arc and iron,
While neon arrow leaps, and electric fish
Bubble a tumult of rockets—oh, the moon, the moon
Is no great ghost now all the lights are on,
But a tin skull, a dead disc in the sky,
An old prop on a worn curtain believed by no one.
Yet suddenly there, waiting in dark rooms,
It compels the hand from habit of the lightswitch—
Commands the windowglass haunting the floor,

A glowing shape of silence breathing in sleep.
Neither now nor ever was it held in the hands—
Cousin of water; symbol of love.—Not anyone's hands.

VI

The pathways in that garden we had known
So long that we could walk them in the night,
And often did; and if sometimes by moonlight
Sometimes not even by star; they overgrown
In massive morning or made small at noon
Or tall and sweet at evening, or deep in fall,
In winter strange as though not there at all
Yet vexed by spring assumed the summer sun.
Time-drifted, war-driven from that place,
Map scrapped, no trains, no tickets to be bought
Back to those arbors, we are not only lost—
Not even together, as though we were untaught
In mutual language and own no common ghost.
I stare at you and almost know your face.

VII

I watched the sea for hours blind with sun,
Hours and hours: all morning a dozen years
Racing and spent in the combers and beyond
Blown back in spume and seagulls' wings and still
Farther ash in the sky, shadowed then lost;
Wind-plowed-over the waves kept rolling in
Lashing salt air cold about my head,
Till the great wave where I saw all my dead
One moment as it stood and they within
As in dark glass which suddenly sun-crossed
Blazed with that luminosity which will

With first or last light raise all things in round
But far and foreign as though seen through tears
Once and forever before the wave shut down.

VIII

When we were children we got too much love,
Grew learned to receive it not to give,
Grow now to face each other with our hope,
At best with nameless name deny ourselves.
Busy with what we do, yet still we wait
And listen for the falling of the sky,
Half aware all murder is suicide,
Knowing at last death easier than love.
In times like these we do the best we can,
In passionate defenses we have trained
To burn each others' cities and to kill
Each others' young. Love is too difficult;
Smoke from enemy capital stinks our beds.
The sky stays; some children may be spared us.

IX

Much has been said of flowers' ignorance:
How in the face of human death and doom,
How in the very road of war's advance,
Violet and buttercup sit out and bloom;
As though they were God's pet extravagance
Morning-glories bugle round a tomb
That knows no Easter; or as to enhance
A night-bombed home, there's cereus in the gloom.
And nations with their troubles will remark
Similarly of stars whose quiet gaze
On love and murder equally lights the dark

With cold contradictions that amaze
The adult race which mostly hesitates to
Destroy a flower, though children often do.

X

"Grandeur is gone, Gogarty, grandeur is gone!"
Cried the old poet in the Dublin garden.
Yet he had come fresh from a grander song
Than any that his young years had heard of.
Grandeur is not within man's keep alone,
Lives neither in great houses nor hard riding.
Grandeur is more likely with the hound,
Most in the hole the fox is hiding in.
Grandeur—that nakedness or that garment
A few young men achieve, some old put on—
From rigidity of conquered torment
Is cut by brain on body's gradual stone;
It is most often where it was least meant,
Most often seen only when the wearer's gone.

X I

(Lie There, My Art)

On you I have continually lusted.
All natural women warm or chill abed
Tired of me, or I of them instead
Of your more dangerous demands, outlasted
By neither night nor sun, that never wasted
You, burning your hands, freezing your head,
Yet all your body ready for me to wed
Elusive thighs, and I the more invested.
Between the world's economy and yours—

The parsimonious spinster's and the whore's—
Must I stay in your sheets until I starve
Or leaving to live return to find you gone?
What madness do you serve that you would have
Me castrate or made impotent as one?

XII

Virgins terrify too many men:
After the preference for the marriage bed
Most are happiest having what's been had,
Lie down easiest where another's been;
They are like clever poets who put in
Their poems snatches out of famous verse
To feel at home with Homer; and of course
To try them backside's just familiar fun;
They are like priests and capitalists and kings
And all too many of the lower class
Who've had each other round so long a time
They do not know how could convenience change
To be desire, desire be love at last;
For they are like the dead, and they are damned.

XIII

Rise up, rise up, Jack Spratt. And you, his wife,
Lie down, lie down to hark the risen cock.
He splits the darkness with his barnyard laugh,
Morning floods in through the simmering crack.
Does the sun drink the dew or earth the sun?—
Hard, hard to tell in all this battering light.
Sun's for singing on, not thinking on;
All's opposite meat and here's the eating of it.
Sure, Jack, you've heard, your nameless wife has heard
The poets and their women cry aloud

That night be long, the moon stay up, day wait
As if love-doings were but night-insured.
But easy folk can rhyme the clock around;
Betwixt the two of them, all opposites meet.

XIV

Then, as 17th century lovers did
Die together—shall we?—and make one
Answer upon our close and private bed
Publicly sworn as our conclusion?
Insurance men and clerks that sit at desks
Computing how to live, retire and die,
Who shall inherit dollars, lose, take risks,
Let them come study our longevity
Here on this white tablet where we add
One with one and fetch a magic one,
Showing two figures so cunningly wed
Can multiply but make no long division,
Who, subtracted from time's required course,
Die here like the expanding universe.

XV

This is the way we say it in our time
When carnal and unmarried love is meant:
I mean we do not make the double back,
Or die: we sleep together. We conjugate
Illegal love—half angel and half crime—
In very verb the least of its intent
For shame of the Elizabethan crack;
Nor are we suicidally elate.
This is the way we compromise, my dear,
Between sweet midnight and the common day,
Remembering we are what other people hear,

What other people and ourselves may say.
This is the way—and let it be a warning—
We wash our hands so early in the morning.

XVI

I questioned the sky: if it were still hollow
And got from the shell of night the old answer
And heard the wave of the day far on the endless
Curve of hidden shore swelling and breaking;
And of the earth: if it were rich or fallow
Spending such flowers from so many bones, or
Ejaculating and eating itself were mindless,
And saw only an endless sleeping and waking.
I thought, if there is power and glory forever,
At most to each of us once, and then only
That moment in the sun's searchlight—in that while
I turn to you, you turn to me, and never
Weep for the night, but as if we were not lonely
Take hands; as if we were one, lie down and smile.

XVII

What happens is, that you are not alone.
Can you understand that?—you are not alone.
Amazement at so much that perishes.
Wonder at what grows large—the two of you.
The soul's "perpetual virginity"
Is lanced and let, even. And the body's
Rearing hunger feeding on itself
Is hungry still; but you do not starve.
You do not cry out—you are very quiet.
At last you are very quiet. Then you turn
And look straight at everything there is

And everybody there is, for the first time.
You know that you can take whatever you will
And leave whatever you will. It is all right.

XVIII

I want to show you a young girl in an orchard
Face down to a book, hair fallen forward,
The May apples' shift of white and green
Lifted around her, sun let out and in;
Such day as you may remember for unnameable
Fragrance and the long slow sound of it all,
As though it were the unopened heart of summer
Somehow known. The girl is at its center.
She is out of herself into the book,
And she and the book and the day together make
A page that holds the sun, and may be so
Forever but that of course I cannot show you
Or know myself. But I can look as long
As I grow older, and none of this will move or change.

XIX

The hour is late, and more for me than you.
Darker then for you? Lighter for me?
Or both? Neither free
But to do singly whatever we must do.
We are alike in that our bones show through
Our thin skins. And let us agree
To spare the legend of our common country
That speaks us cold: let strangers think it true.
The torment burns. Be near me still, or far,
You like a lean Egyptian pace my mind—
And where were other breasts savage as these?

111

Forehead dramatized with visible scar?
I grow so willful as to think to find
Somewhere doubtless there is a place of peace.

X X

These words may be a dress for you to wear
While you walk forever in the sun;
Or at the least the ribbon in your hair
To bind it that it never be undone.
—So big and little poets usually cry
In anguished boast that none of them can lose
Nor the world lose this one girl; and so I,
Bringing you here in your embroidered shoes.
You, like all the others, shall grow old
And die; words shaped on your young body
May be as mortal as your flesh and cold
As only time could teach you how to be.
The fierce completion of your nakedness
Makes death unnecessary and this dress.

X X I

Your hair, for the first time a concern
Of someone in the night, diffused about me:
Flowers more known than seen and yet that burn.
Now I know how golden this will be—
As gold as I remember it to be.
Possessed or unpossessed, it is all one—
Though dangerous difference enough to me—
Winter daffodils, and a midnight sun.
Lie in my arms, my love, a little while,
As though it were forever, for it is;
There is no difference. And you can guess,

So young, my answer to my question while
I hardly need to tell you what it is.
Am I your father, brother, lover? Yes.

XXII

I write who on this night four weeks ago
Sleeping held you sleeping even till morning.
You see now what I am, what monstrous thing
I am that so can batten even on you.
Even I beneath the memory of that night
Stare for dumb, helpless hours; but at least
I am that creature cursed, blessed, diseased
With words—at most I turn again and write.
Other men have loved and other women
Have been beautiful; may even be
Have loved as much as I and looked like you.
It yet is news, and a necessity
In bitter times to publish it as true,
My mistress' hair is something like the sun.

XXIII

I almost thought I saw us on the stair
Of stone between the two streets—halfway up
Where the trumpet vine spills over from the top,
The dark step of the deepest shadows there;
But nobody was there where once we were
Unless it was our ghosts I almost saw,
Some gesture of mine that escaped time's law,
Your suddenly lifted head of famous hair.
Or do the live have ghosts? I do not know.
It was not April sunlight any more
That lay below, above the stair of stone;

A desolate, hotter, emptier, July glow
That burned and smarted like a feverish sore.
But I went up, somehow not alone.

XXIV

Take my hand. Your hand was chill as mine.
Now both are warmed. So. We draw apart
From others. Our intent is isolation
If necessary. But everybody, every street
Is beautiful. At once. We touch the world.
This immense tenderness. Why, this
Would be the way, wouldn't it! Go out
By going in. Go everywhere, coming close.
The hands are only ours. Touch everywhere,
Birthmark and childhood scar. Also
Hidden somewhere, tissue of death growing.
Go little that tragedy—it sweetens us.
Now we are awake. We know. We are.
We warm the sun. We have invented spring.

XXV

The hour is short, wisdom is very hard—
The birth, though love, is long: it hurts, it hurts.
Pain, that we so prayed we might be spared,
Is now the clawing captive of our hearts.
But those who look away from it go blind.
We are what we can look upon and know.
There is no sin but Lot's wife's who sinned
By turning and denying what she saw.
Between the worm and mastery of heaven
We hung for mad. Because the hour is short
O let us endlessly believe our end
Is in ourselves, as earth's within the earth.

Earth, teach us to care, teach us to move,
To change, assent to seasons, even to love.

XXVI

Leave over-loving (but leave ignorance,
Take questioning and knowledge) of the earth,
Where our first questions went, where all our answers
Gather upon the day that takes us down.
Here are no human voices for our hope
And let none be imagined, but grave peace
Speaks over living sweat its lucid air
—Less than we asked and more than all our lives.
There is no tower here but that one grace
To undo our scattered towers, bolt and stone;
This heave of grass and thrust of blossoming branch
Takes enemies' allegiance every one
And every loving face, and even now
Speaks over us the peace that needs no hands.

Heterocercy

I recall my first grown spring
That horned me with love:
After the furtive wonders
The search, the moonraker lust:
Recall it—vague, simple year—
As a legend of hope lost,
The boy a ghost, his unicorn
Haunting undiscovered canyons
Seen in my mind, that knows
Too well the complex heart

The too seldom ravished flesh:
That sees me, though a young man,
Foolish in my plain desire
As it were an old man's nonsense
To go daggered in modern dress.

Flowering Quince

If right in front of me,
Slow motion—fast motion really—
The cold branch of the quince
Should all at once
Start with a rash of buds
Then the thin green nudge
The brown back, then the color
Of the waxen flower, the flame,
Open everywhere the same
Golden-centered swirl
Of odor, sweet burning odor—
Performed in one day, one hour
Or even one minute
Which would then hold in it,
For more than sense or praise
Could say, all April's days—
That would set my heart awhirl.
This stratagem
Of instant gold from green
I have never seen
On tree or branch or stem:
Never never never—only once;
Once, and it was a girl.

Green and Red and Darkness

For twenty minutes between the end of storm
And the last of sunset, green became green and
All red roses stepped forward a little and burned.

Then from all over the world like an
Indeterminate number of dusk-robed figures
Evening walked to the center and made darkness.

And then it was my ancestors, for they said
"Now you have all the stars, surer than roses."
"Damn you," I said: "damn you, you dead dead."

To Marry Strangers

Since after all we were born to marry strangers—
O child, child, child that I never knew!—
Is this photograph of a child I have begotten
And forgotten? Or is it you?

                              Or is it true
Love alive is no more retroactive
Than sure of any future? But though it may
Imagine you both beautiful and gray
Cannot, the other way, return and find you?
Where would it find you? This child, this
Beloved stranger? Unconceived daughter? Who?

This is wild—this riddles reason,
This leap of leaves storming off the ground—
Their turning from gold to green is wild
Yet I love this child—would go to her, hold her—
Wherever she could be found.

                        But no, but no:
The leaves are never still, they fall all seasons.
And none, none, none resumes the bough.
That alone which is lost will find what is lost,
And you are here, and I: and in this noon
Not even small ghosts run. Across the sun
No voice bends back the wind. But always the wind
Lifts your hair and all the sun is shaken,
And yet may lift it colorless in the moon,
And I—in so much blest—alone remember
The light that moves upon your strange face now.

Innumerable Death

I am these days much distracted by death:
By count of war, innumerable death. I
Am a stranger at too many funerals, and grief
Impersonal as rain that slows the night
That nobody had noticed when it began
Goes on repeating midnight hour by hour, and I
Grow much preoccupied by death, everywhere.

That it is not mine to know, nor mine to die:
I have not died at Stalingrad or home,
Having bequeathed that lie in another life.
Neither is my own death my distraction.

I talked my death to death many years ago in
The sunlight somewhere. I was very young.
What was I saying? Not this general cold rain.

Where there were bones and violets and peace
Death moved in Act the Fifth, the curtain fell,
I rose from him to acknowledge the applause;
Or if he came to the house, there equally known
As one familiar with our ceremonies, often
Seen at the neighbors', with private meaning.—
Peace be with violets now, bones and the sun.

I am distracted by this shapeless death that
Has taken all the air, grown out of his name.
Even if he turns upon me my friends' faces
For me to see white in the endless rain,
What shall I call him? Even this autumn now
Loosening out to the long fall of leaves
Darkens for nothing that it ever was.

Endless Cypress

When will I wish so much to see them again as to believe that
    I shall?
When will I persuade spring to persuade me that there arise and
    return
A personal dandelion and an individual daffodil? When,
O my dead, must I say to the grass and the dirt: We are different
    from you?

He I heard die, she I watched die, and she whose body I found,
    and those

Old or young who died long after I saw them but died, all, too
   soon—
Ah, was there none I loved enough to make me believe the earth
   had shut in vain?
If so, then what bearable love could I know that would betray
   me yet into that?

Spring and summer and fall and winter and day and night and
   each other;
Our imperfection seeds all our desire and necessitates all our art;
   and death
Is not the begetter of sorrow, and grief is for its own sake or the
   song it makes;
Walking always toward the endless cypress, this side of it all are
   beautiful and dear.

Journal Note

I dreamed I saw Thomas Hardy. I woke up
To the sound of soldiers singing in the street,
Marching, and singing together an endless song
That ran wistfully lightly over the boot beat.

I stood alone, naked at the window and looked down:
Helmet and pack, the identical boy kept passing.
I had stood just now in the sun at the sea edge.
Ting-ling-ling-ling. I buy her everything

To keep her in style. Better days are coming by and by.
I had stood just now in the sun at the sea edge,
I said to the girl beside me, my mouth on her hair,
"Isn't it wonderful he lives on and on to such age!"

There was the little old man like a little old gray bird
With bright quick eyes, and I held the girl to me so
All her slight weight was a sweet agony of peace.
She was younger than I. Without moving she answered "No."

I stood alone, naked at the window and looked down,
For the drumming boots and the song with its running-bell sound.
Blue flashed up out of the yard and dazzled my eyes:
Morning-glories and not, as I first thought, something beyond.

The U.S. Sailor with the Japanese Skull

Bald-bare, bone-bare, and ivory yellow: skull
Carried by a thus two-headed U.S. sailor
Who got it from a Japanese soldier killed
At Guadalcanal in the ever-present war: our

Bluejacket, I mean, aged 20, in August strolled
Among the little bodies on the sand and hunted
Souvenirs: teeth, tags, diaries, boots; but bolder still
Hacked off this head and under a Ginkgo tree skinned it:

Peeled with a lifting knife the jaw and cheeks, bared
The nose, ripped off the black-haired scalp and gutted
The dead eyes to these thoughtful hollows: a scarred
But bloodless job, unless it be said brains bleed.

Then, his ship underway, dragged this aft in a net
Many days and nights—the cold bone tumbling
Beneath the foaming wake, weed-worn and salt-cut
Rolling safe among fish and washed with Pacific;

Till on a warm and level-keeled day hauled in
Held to the sun and the sailor, back to a gun-rest,
Scrubbed the cured skull with lye, perfecting this:
Not foreign as he saw it first: death's familiar cast.

Bodiless, fleshless, nameless, it and the sun
Offend each other in strange fascination
As though one of the two were mocked; but nothing is in
This head, or it fills with what another imagines

As: here were love and hate and the will to deal
Death or to kneel before it, death emperor,
Recorded orders without reasons, bomb-blast, still
A child's morning, remembered moonlight on Fujiyama:

All scoured out now by the keeper of this skull
Made elemental, historic, parentless by our
Sailor boy who thinks of home, voyages laden, will
Not say, "Alas! I did not know him at all."

MR. WHITTIER AND OTHER POEMS (1948)

Mr. Whittier

It is so much easier to forget than to have been Mr. Whittier.
Though of course no one now remembers him when he was young.
A few old ladies who were little girls next door in Amesbury,
Or practically next door, have reminiscences of pears and apples
Given them by the famous, tamed, white-bearded saint with the
Still inextinguishable dark Hebraic eyes; and
Of course there is the old man—and I for one am grateful—who
Recalls the seedy coat, the occasionally not so clean high collar,
And that like many another he read his paper by the hour in the
    privy.
Carl Schurz, finding him rained in by the stove at the village store,
Thought "So superior to those about him, and yet so like them";
    and
His official biographer decided that Mr. Whittier's poetry was the
    kind
"Written first of all for the neighbors." There are lesser and worse.

In any case, here is a city, founded in 1630, present population
    somewhere about
55,000—has been more in boom times, and has been a lot less;—
    say,
In three hundred years has birthed a couple of hundred thousand
    people
And one poet. Not bad. And as proof of the title I shall only
    remark
It is easier to leave *Snow-Bound* and a dozen other items in or out
    of
The school curriculum than it is to have written them. Try it and
    see.

Born where the east wind brought the smell of the ocean from
    Plum Island up-river,
At a brookside haunted in the foggy dark of autumn nights
By six little witches in sky-blue capes—Uncle Moses had seen
    them;—
Born on a farm to the *Bible, Pilgrim's Progress,* a weekly paper,
    the Quaker meeting-house,
To hard poverty, obscure, and a few winters of country school;
To die—though only after there were thirteen for dinner, and the
    clock
Suddenly stopped—ancient with fame, with honorary degrees, and
One hundred thousand dollars all made out of poems—I say
Even this was not easy, though also it is not
What I am talking about, but is really incidental along with
Not liking Walt Whitman and never quite affording marriage.

Neither, under the circumstances, could it have been easy, and it
    was important,
To stand suddenly struck with wonder of old legends in a young
    land,
To look up at last and see poetry driving a buckboard around the
    bend,
And poetry all the time in the jays screeching at the cats in the
    dooryard,
Climbing with the thrush into the August noon out of the boy's
    sight
As he dawdled barefoot through poetry among the welts of the
    goldenrod;
But nothing is hardest which treads on nobody else's toes.

Let us not begrudge Mr. Whittier his white beard, his saintliness,
    his other foibles;
Let us remember him when he was young, not to begrudge his rise
As a goddam Abolitionist hated not only in the South,
Hated by manufacturers, politicians, the neighbors, our folk, all

Who hate the outspoken radical and know a safer way;
Denounced by the clergy—a serious matter in that time; by the
    good men who
Rotten-egged him in New Hampshire, burned him out in Pennsyl-
    vania,
Jailed those who read him, and twenty years later immortally froze
With Webster on whom he turned his scorn of compromise.
It is so much easier to forget than to have been Mr. Whittier.

He put the names of our places into his poems and he honored us
    with himself;
And is for us but not altogether, because larger than us.
When he was an old man, the Negroes came to him free to come
    and sang to him
"The Lord bless thee and keep thee;
The Lord make his face to shine upon thee and be gracious unto
    thee;
The Lord lift up his countenance upon thee, and give thee peace."
—No more begrudge their freedom than his tears.

"After Great Pain a Formal Feeling Comes"
(Emily Dickinson)

What is rejected becomes a greater thing.
All things referred draw drama from its size.
So Amherst can become the fabulous sun,
One yard a kingdom and one house a castle,
One room a throne, and dry within that room
One closet be the casket of a name.

Call Emily. And fetch a mischievous dance
Of petals and butterflies and bees turned stars

Turned fireflies between the hedge and window
Where the girl in the white dress glimmers and goes.
Offstage, the larger terror than we want
Save in the larger eyes of those returned.

But there's a dance—a ballet of Emily:
A thousand of her in pirouetting white
Like great revolving daisies all the way
From her father's door over into the graveyard—
A gay haunting in the middle of town.
Then as in a movie this dissolves.

Speak to the stone and to the grass and to the door:
Where is Emily? The Sabbath noon
It still and empty, or is only still,
Or is not even quite exactly still.
By such singleness is singularity
Made multiple, and Emily everywhere.

She knows now the necessity to deny
The Father, Son, but never the Holy Ghost.
She weds the Holy Ghost and it is death—
A going down under the garden beds
And then a resurrection as if alone;
The mountain of darkness taken into her.

Only through denial great acceptance
As only in depths of silence the tall song:
She walks here as immortal as the light—
Made indistinguishable from the air,
Having the self-possession of the sun.
Emily becoming Emily forever.

Wilson

We walked with him in the rain, road after road,
But each time we came to the place we were alone,
We would not go in; and we turned alone with the words.

Abandoned far behind us the room was a ruin
Of tumbled desks, split books, and faded maps;
Only the schoolmaster's voice sternly repeating
Repeating whatever we still had strength to hear.
We turned and turned beneath words and could never hide.
But when we followed and came to the place we would not go in.

We returned to the bright and easy fields of the country;
For thunderous hours the shadows of planes passed over us
Multitudinous crosses. Then in the hollowed silence
The voice began again repeating the words and the place.

His was the only conspicuous defeat, the only defeat of importance.
Our enemies' defeat and our victory were the same.
They believed in the body's resurrection as performance of the
    worshiped body,
What had failed should be made larger, the goldener calf.

When at last we came to the place he could not go in;
He who came down from the mountain with the law
Yet led us on past the shattered slates, knowing the pieces
No more than his broken body—receptacle merely:
Henceforth the words informed and survived in our flesh,
Woke and arose in the bodies of our enemies, or did not live;
Knowing the teacher is never the ultimate participant,
The wage of his vision is death, is not to cross over.

We walked with him in the rain, road after road.
Would the breaking of his body be sufficient
If through crack of the bones the quickened spirit
Struck sun broad upon land that lay ahead?
The voice repeated, repeated that this was the way.
When we came at last to the place he was there before us.

May 1506

Christopher Columbus speaking:

I do not want your praises later on.
When I am dead I shall rest easier
In lack of borrowed breathing; and you will
Be tempted—never doubt—to sweeten up
Your own names with the fame of praising mine.
Even your scoffing mouths that so reviled me
Can learn again the shape of knew-him-when
And claim a talking share in India.

I began beggar and I finish beggared—
Beggared of gold and trumpets and renown
That Spain one moment lent me. It is nothing.
The unpaid tavern bill, the leaking roof
I would bequeath to later dangerous men
As their insurance of a happy death.

Feed on my bones if that will make you fat,
I can't prevent your feast; but all that marrow
Shall not fetch you memory of those beaches
And how they glittered beyond the tired sails.
Beggared I am but never of that look.
O rebels, traitors, slanderers, embezzlers

Who stole and lied to get me rags and chains!
I had my strength, but yours was cleverness;
Yet mine that troubles you the most, the longest.

God forgive me. Christ save the King and Queen
To whom I freely will all India.
I was no longer young when I first voyaged
And I was old and gutted at the last.

How did I harm you? Was my fame my crime?
Did my light, coruscant light of a new land
That was to shine for all, diminish yours?
Or did you think a feeding claw could hold it—
The gold—this side the King and the Word of God?
In that great wake beneath the foreign stars
What little Caesars sailed the charted course
And swarmed like eager spiders on the treasure
As though they could not wait to make it ruin—
That I had looked upon to name and bless.

Viceroy of India, Admiral of the Seas.
I wrap my names about me like old flags
That have had honor once, as well you know.
My grave has room for them and truth and me.
Cape Gracios à Dios and Veragua,
Andalusia's long way to Española,
Farthest-followed sun and under it
The curve of surf falling forward west.
Why did you hate my finding India?

Gert Swasey

Have you ever asked yourselves—ladies, ladies—what it must have
    been like
To have been Gert Swasey?
To have a rich father,
To run away from home
To be a circus queen, and
To come back a charlady?
To come home and be old?
Dirty and old?

Few of you now can remember Gert Swasey
When she was young—how she was young:
What was it like do you suppose
To drive through town as though you thumbed your nose,
Your red hair flying, and beautiful clothes?
What was it like to want to do that
Seventy years ago—ladies, ladies?
Gert was a wild one, and when she wanted
She'd drive a pair of horses like a witch enchanted.
She'd drive them down from Mount Washington
As though she were fired out of a cannon;
And all the way along Merrimac,
Up Main, through Summer Street, down Mill and back
Till she charged up the driveway of her father's mansion,
Twice around where the iron stag stared,
Then as fast to the coach-house as she dared
Which was twice as fast as anybody dared;
The horses snorting and all in lather,
But there was nothing Gert would rather

Than set the whole downtown awhirl
Gasping at that Swasey girl.

I wonder how it was to be that Swasey girl
Not a Sanders nor a Dow nor a Saltonstall,
But new-rich Irish with no family at all
Save a sporting father who kept a stable.
It must have been both mad and sweet
To thunder through leaf-filled Summer Street
Disturbing the ladies at the tea table,
Disturbing the ladies in the summer house,
And all along Merrimac's shops and factories
The men's quick faces.

Then to run away—to run far away
To ride in a circus—
The colored wheels
The tights and spangles
The lights, the crowd
The wonderful horses,
The plumed, proud, wonderful white horses,
The tremendous music.
To travel like a gypsy
To dress like a queen
To see all the world that she'd never seen
That was never the world where she had been.
Not a Dow nor a Sanders nor a Saltonstall
Unless they paid to get in.
And then
After thirty-five years to come home again.

Have you ever asked yourselves what it must have been like
To be the old charlady at the B. & M. railroad station?
To clean the toilets
To mop the floors

To be greasy and gray
To be poor and alone
To be Gert Swasey?
Then there is a way—easy to learn—
Of talking to yourself,
Answering yourself,
When there is no one else
Wherever you are.
There are many stray cats, a dozen—fifty—
That will stay in your house
If you will feed them,
Lock them in to keep them safe,
Whose yowling some day wakes the neighborhood
But, at last, not you.

Have you ever asked yourselves what it must have been like
To have been Gert Swasey?
To be a rich young nobody with red restless hair?
To run away from home
To be a circus queen, and
To come back,
And to be old, and to be dirty, and to be dead—
O, ladies, ladies.

Winslow Homer

Fog. He can see only this deep still fog.
Roweled by the falling sun it smoulders westward awhile
But it closes impenetrable curtains: night is fleshed.
No shore, save for the long jut of staggered rock
Shelving a black sharp stair to the burdened, hidden sea.
This he paints in his old age, recording his utter love.

For him there is one canvas, thick with seventy years—
Picture over picture buried, each worked from the last.
Where are the children's faces in the morning schoolroom?
Far under battlefields of the Civil War,
Eaten out by tenser light, man-riddled noon.
Even summer landscape empty kept a memory of people—
Visitors passing and strange. Then one seaman storm-struck.
All vanished now, washed over in a high tide of paint
As though the colors of the world, faster and faster whirling,
Spun this still center of gray; this inevitable mist:
Sun lost, sea filled and covered,
The great stair of black rock deserted, used no more.

Hamlet and Hamlet
Elsinore: A Platform Before the Castle.
Midnight. Two Ghosts:

HAMLET

Though I am dead, oh I am haunted still.
Mortmain—mortmain: upon me even now?
Does that same hand which pulled me toward my grave
Yet drag me out of it for further death?

KING

I am your father, Hamlet. Would I be sane
Being both your begetter and your slayer?

HAMLET

How should I know, who will not have a son.
Yours may have been a madness kept for kings—
That, too, I'll never know. And then again
It may be general between here and hell
If one has left a hostage in his name

To work it out. Who's marked for murder now
That, though the dirt is not dry over me
And no stone tells the place among so many
All newly dug, you call me back again
Against the midnight and the westward star?
Is any left to kill? I learned the dead
Can kill: but not each other.

KING

                              Hamlet,
As far as death is kindlier than life
I'd hoped to find the dead forgive the dead.

HAMLET

Odd words from you. I take them for a father's.

KING

Listen, my son: wind rises and far down
The sea is thrashing higher, for the world
Turns toward the steeper east. The brightening stars
Flash inward their corroborative sign
That they have little time. And you and I
Are left with what they have before the cock
Cries up the light that washes us away—
Our quarreling white shadows both dissolved
Into the sun's decision. We shall die
Wholly and rest if we can find our peace.
Can we not pause for that and then forever?

HAMLET

I see a sort of peace around us here:
Dark—dark and all but toppling with the dead
Who did not ask for this. My wretched uncle
Who killed you for the power and the Queen
And got them and drew all this after them—

Whose blessing did he have before your curse?
Why was he let? And wasn't that enough?
See how revenge upon him caught us all—
Pompous Polonius and, son for son,
Laertes and myself—and from that poison
Another potion for the Queen; and from
My feigning madness real for Ophelia.
All dead and gone. Inside these walls which gleam
And shudder in the imperturbable light
Of those unstaying stars, all strangers now.
All strange. All ruin. All silence. Is that peace?

      KING
So ends the world.

      HAMLET
                Was it thus ordained?
Tell me: were you privy to God's book?
Did you foresee the slaughter, now return
For one last look upon it and to bless it?
Ah, did you—tell me!—did you will my death?

      KING
O Hamlet, Hamlet! Evil that struck me down,
Evil that emerged from the same womb
Which dropped me, forming me a righteous man,
Had seized the realm in which you were beloved,
Entered the very body of your mother.
It was as though a part of my own blood
Blackened with infection yet could be
Knifed out and spare the whole to heaven again.

      HAMLET
And in the cutting what a wound was made!
That large it bled a kingdom.

KING
                              At my death
You mourned me with such passion of despair,
More even than is dutiful in sons,
I thought you were in love with death itself
And courting it.

HAMLET
                    Yes, so I almost won.
I lost a father but I was no father.
I got a father who could not be mine:
So lost my mother. Then I gained a ghost.

KING
But if I gloved my dead hand within yours—
As though a virtuous Abel might avenge
Through his regeneration murderous Cain
By a reversal on him of his act,—
I thought as much to move the death in you
Outward against its source and cleanse you of it.
Alas, the sword is colored by its thrust.

HAMLET
Whom did I move against? I never knew.
Whenever I put my hand upon the hilt
It weighed as though I hefted up my heart.
And when I drew at last upon Laertes
Who crossed me as the slayer of his father
I might have been his uncle, or my own.
Who was I then? Where could I find myself?

KING
That was the burden which you would not bear.
I had forgot how slim a boy you were
When, right or wrong, I married you to murder.

My death that should have manned you in my place
Made you a gelding with a memory
Hot, confused, by turns afraid and vile.

HAMLET
Ah, you accuse me still!

KING
                                   Some fault was mine.
Death does not cloak us in a wise man's magic,
But in these days while dissolution wears
Slowly upon us until we are gone—
As even now we two await the sun
Which soon all air will breathe to filling flame—
We watch awhile. Perhaps in recollection
Of others or ourselves we stay awhile
Gazing upon it all. Not wholly judge.
As if the phosphorent flesh itself remember
Though but an iridescent failing vapor
The shape of hand, the murmur of the pulse.
For we are never utterly purified
Out of that flesh till we are gone too far
To know or care, even to recall our names.
Interval of intelligence remains
Between the midnight and the foreign morning
That lights another history on the earth
In which we are a scattered, nameless dust.
Interval of the echoing of love
Possible only in the living body,
In us withdrawing homeward to the sun.
We are its lingering music. Mine the sin
That in this over-lengthened interval,
Made powerful by my willing and your wanting,
I sought to heat this to a vengeful brand
And marked you wickedly.

139

HAMLET

Oh, Father! Father!
Why was I not smothered in your death?
Half-breathing, half-awake; why was I left
A dreaming paralytic—too afraid
To follow and too dispossessed to stay?

KING

There was the halfway that you tried to take,
Like a tall dancer spinning mad between
Earth and sky in alternate aversion.
All believed but you and so you failed.

HAMLET

Laertes played my braver self. I thought:
If his blade overpower mine, it's mine.
We fused from common cause a common end,
And where we fell lay double suicide.

KING

And who was Prince that day?

HAMLET

Why, there was none
Because there was no King in Elsinore.

KING

My brother Claudius was king enough.
All had their death before he suffered his.
Polonius—

HAMLET

I speared him in the dark,
Thinking him greater fish.

140

KING

Perhaps. Ophelia—

HAMLET

Never my wish! All my desire! O death,
Grave magician of zeros out of zero!

KING

The Queen—

HAMLET

Another's accident.

KING

Laertes—

HAMLET

Most deliberate and least intentioned.
My own scratch opened first.

KING

And then the King!
What a mound of carcase you bestrode
Before you stood up tall enough to reach
Into his heart! And then the thrust that got him
Seemed your arm's involuntary twitch.
Dying, you touched him cold.

HAMLET

My lord forgets
The last news that I had: my mother's death,
The poison on my sword. And then I stood.
And then I was alone. And then I moved.

141

KING

Revenge. My son, it took so long a course
That when it came I wonder whose it was?

HAMLET

Stones rolling down a mountainside: the one
Knocking against the next—so on—till all
Dispersed they lie and quiet at the foot,
With no more morals than the mountainside;
And none can tell the first stone from the last.
Cleaner the mountain stands, but who's to say
How much, or what the difference is in that?
Oh, I am getting weary for my grave.
I would be carried like a little boy
And put to bed again; for I am tired
Of all the toys of death. Where is the morning
That is my night? The starlight worries me
As though the world had stopped and heaven were fixed,
Trigged here forever with us—and no story
Save one, and none to tell it but myself;
It sickens me and will not make me sleep.
I'm cold.

KING

Translucent pictures of my arms
That once when stout for pleasure of the task
Sometimes when you were small did nurse's work;
So warm a weight your head against my shoulder
I would delay upon the corridor
Or carry you the long way to your room,
Wishing I knew a song.

HAMLET

I don't remember.
Look! Does the east show there a milky line?

KING

It cracks a little I think that side of the sea.
The cock will spy it first. Trust him to warn
The world into its flesh again and blast us
Out of our tranced adventure. Peter heard it
Twice before he knew how cold was truth.

HAMLET

I wish I might have Peter's knowledge now.

KING

Never, until after Peter's sorrow;
And then no man can tell you truth from tears.

HAMLET

Then I betrayed you? Speak!

KING

                    You are not Peter.
Had you betrayed yourself—then me also.
But self-deception you could not contrive.
In desperate reasoning to be free you tried.
And yet you could not.

HAMLET

                  I cast this way and that.
As though I tossed in chains. It was the vow.
You swore me to swear vengeance on your death
And then the death was hung on me like iron.
I rattled with it every step I took.
I stopped and waited—then would step again—
This way and that—not quite believing it
Unless I moved—and then all frigid horror.
Everywhere there was no one but I.
And everywhere I could not find myself.

A ring of mirrors of my own invention—
I wheeled among them searching for a door.

KING

I think no exit gave except this one.
We walk tonight across that shattered glass
Hearing the crunch and tinkle of those deaths
As though some pretty instrument were smashed
Which once made music; now beneath our feet
Glint scattered, dimmer than most distant stars,
But with the question if they had to be.

HAMLET

I said your ghost was Satan up from hell
Arrayed in father's guise to purchase me.
Then proved it false.

KING

                           Almost against your hope.

HAMLET

Had you been King of hell and not of Denmark
I'd been relieved of murder. I had grief
Enough to weigh me down.

KING

                           When I returned
I was a king of moonlight armed with shade,
The cold reflection of the day. O night
That trembles now at pressure of this dawn
Bring back once more my scepter, make me king
Of anything—of waves, winds, rocks, myself,
Of Hamlet even!

HAMLET

Your name and mine are one.

KING

My shadow fought to lodge within your flesh—
Assume your blood and bone, inhabit you
With my avenging ghost, take on your warmth,
To be another Hamlet, be my son.

HAMLET

To make me King and father, yet myself?
Then who was Prince and who was in his court?
What thing upon the throne? Whose Queen in bed?
Who was beloved Ophelia if not Queen?
How was the Queen another but my mother?
What scarred Ophelia then? How could I love?
How could I kill? Oh, I inherited
A scrambled madness of incestuous nightmare
In which the faces interchanged—the play
Went wildly round and round before a throne
On which there sat a king as heretofore,
Who still embraced my mother and who grinned
Like a conspiratorial daddy, winking
To bid me share the gaiety, put off
The black reminder I had had a father,
Or I had been a son. Who was I then?
Who was I if not Hamlet, Prince of Denmark,
Nor Hamlet, King of Denmark? Was I both?
Then damned and double damned to work it out—
The live avenger and the dead betrayed:
Joined confusions and impossible
Yet joined indeed.

KING

My son, forgive my hands
That are a scattering smoke, blown mist through which

Even paler starlight shines to show
How emptied of all human heat they are,
Being no longer useful to take others'
Or touch a head or beat upon the air
Because what most they loved has now become
As thin a ghost as they, and by their guilt.
Since now in death we are indeed as one,
In these last moments listen to me, Hamlet,
And grant it stay the memory of my voice
As you have loved it best, if you can love
Even my name, which is your name, again.

HAMLET
I hear you still.

KING
                    In life we are as one
But not in undifferentiated death.
I sought to enter the forbidden way.
I strove to make you proxy of my seed
But not to sow a life. I should have known
That witling Claudius my surviving self—
I, shorn of all but lust for Queen and power,
Dead-ended, that was I upon the throne,
And death was there and would have been enough.
If anyone was Satan it was he—
Not up from hell but fallen out of heaven
With his ambition round him like a net
Certain to choke him. All my sins upon him
Save sharp resentment of accomplishment
That should have seen his victory too rotted
Long to sustain its hour. But forth I drove you
As my begotten son to teach revenge.
And it was that you wrestled to betray.
I staked my death in you. You fought. The death

Was never yours until the end. I see
Your life was mine but only if it lived.
Out of mine but broken off—not leashed
For an incredulous continuance.
My more would be your less—your less my loss—
And thus it was. See now what I have done!

HAMLET

Ah! but it's over save the sound of it
Upon Horatio's tongue and a few more
Who will report these things and fix the blame
A dozen ways by Sunday and forget
By Monday. We are through with all of that.
Evil will call up evil on itself
Without the intercession of the dead,
And our tried remedy of self-destruction
Will not be questioned—old authorities
Are all with you and me. Laertes, dying,
Taught me my text as I outwaited him—
He gave me his forgiveness and took mine
Which now I understand and would bestow
On my beloved father; which to give
Is most to have and keep. And, oh, this peace
In my own name upon us all.

KING

                    —The cock!
Hear how he kindles on the day's new hearth.

HAMLET

Fade, Father! And so I! Leave light to earth.

Definition

This habit of avoiding unpleasantness: it avoids
Poetry, it avoids love; which is to say it brings
Dissimilarities together without revelation;
It is a sodomy; it chooses, in the long run, war.

It bears both a lily and a gun; an idiot, it
Crazes all conversation in its neighborhood and falsifies
The air we breathe. Indeed, it is against air. It distrusts
The sun. To worship death, to endure itself, it invents God.

The Ivory Bed

Who has not beheld fair Venus in her pride
Of nakedness, all alabaster white,
In Ivory bed, strait laid by Mars his side,
And hath not been enchanted by the sight?
                                    —GEORGE PEELE

The treading pigeon arcs his wings
As though his love were sped with flight,
And muscular with morning flings
The slated sunrise out of night.

Below him in the public square
The sailor, soldier, and marine
Get up and go away to war
From copulation on the Green.

148

Strange girls get up and go away.
In grass beneath the General—
Immortal bronze assured on clay—
Death's flat and rubber fingers fall.

That generation drains to grass
Without the twenty years' delay
In which to learn for what it was.
So peace begins the winsome day.

Pvt. John Hogg

In the war—oh, not the last war nor the one before—this was
Eighty-odd years ago and nobody now—the Civil War—

I can see— the way it still—beyond the white picket fence the little
    white farmhouse and the door
Open to June sun—the terrible way the young man left—leaped out
Between the rusted lilac and the yellow roses and ran up the road.

Did his wife with the baby girl, the boy clutched at her apron,
    follow to the dooryard?
I think so—but of course now nobody—though I am sure his father
    sat alone in the house;
And his mother—this is what I was told—what I know—lay across
    the doorsill: why he leaped that way that day.
Because she had said over and over "Don't—don't—don't" and
"If you go it will be over my body."

Wind running the sun in the trees and the short beat of his
    running up the summer road and gone,
Oh, it is so long ago and now there's nobody saw him and nobody
    sees him but me; and there's nothing.

It was all for nothing—running through the sweet dust to his death
    in a fevered bed off New Orleans harbor.
Nobody has anything now of his except some blood.

Three American Women and a German Bayonet

Outweighing all, heavy out of the souvenir bundle
The German bayonet: grooved steel socketed in its worn wood
    handle,
Its detached and threatening silence.
Its gun-body lost, the great knife wrested to a personal particular
    violence—
Now bared shamelessly for what it is, here exposed on the
    American kitchen table and circled with the wreath
Of his three women, the hard tool of death.

And while Mary his mother says "I do not like it. Put it down"
Mary the young sister, her eyes gleaming and round,
Giddily giggles as, the awkward toy in her left hand,
She makes impertinent pushes toward his wife who stands
Tolerant of child's play, waiting for her to be done.
His mother says "I wish he had not got it. It is wicked-looking. I
    tell you: Put it down!"
His wife says "All right, Mary: let me have it—it is mine."
Saucily pouting, primly frowning
The sister clangs bayonet on table; walks out
And her mother follows.

Like a live thing in not-to-be-trusted stillness,
Like a kind of engine so foreign and self-possessed
As to chill her momently between worship and terror
It lies there waiting alone in the room with her,

Oddly familiar without ever losing strangeness.
Slowly she moves along it a tentative finger
As though to measure and remember its massive, potent length:
Death-deep, tall as life,
For here prized from the enemy, wrenched away captive, his danger-
ous escape and hers.
Mary his wife
Lifts it heavy and wonderful in her hands and with triumphant
tenderness.

Forgive Me, Stranger

Shrive me? Can it be Tuesday now?
Can I be touched, washed, blessed, made whole?
Stayed so on Wednesday? Sir, I fear
Who touches me feels acid; so beware,
And I am cold, sir, also; bitter cold.
You cannot come near if I say you can't,
And you are not the child I put aside;
How can you touch me? In this garden
Are rocks and sand with roses, and beyond it
Spit and nails and vinegar and nothing.
Can you drink night? That gravel pit of stars,
They'd cut and choke you. Better, vinegar
Or even nails and spit; best of all, nothing.
Or could you if my thought believed you could?
No, I will not eat this blackness for you,
For I am cold enough. Go shrive yourself,
And I will lay one hand upon the other
To find if doubled zero makes warm wealth,
Or swallowing my tears turns salt to wine.
I'd heard the child was here who'd comfort me,

Having some wisdom about sleep and singing
Which I've forgot; but you are old and strange,
And no more help to me than I to you.
Forgive me, stranger; and—I'll—oh! my hands!

Day of the Russets

The boy, the man, and the old man in the orchard
Gathered russet apples all day long.

Their feet printed frosty grass of the morning,
Boy's running, man's steady, grandfather's scuff.

The little grove, fragrant with ripened russets,
Took them in just as it took the sun.

Grandfather picked what he reached, father on ladder;
The boy filled burlap from the brown-green ground.

There were big fall-defying bees, I remember,
And grackles that kept sorting the field.

Too fast at first for talk, too tired later,
They worked, and also too much at ease.

Afternoon resumed sound of small punches
Apple by apple now not quite so cold.

But the day grayed with the sun southwest,
Northeast the dull clouds beginning to shut.

The boy quit, to start eating the harvest,
Sitting half asleep except chill hands.

Toward the last, grandfather went picking flowers,
Coming back burdened with asters in the dusk.

My Grandmother Townley's Funeral

The slow procession of old people begins now
Enters now the fragrant room and crossing
Bends with the weight of its own emptiness
And makes a moving scythe toward the open coffin.

Garnering nothing it turns upon itself,
It moves in a measure of pauses, a hesitant
Numbed and ordained last dance, a shuffled grief
Circles like a withering wreath before the dead.

Like understudies of a retiring star,
Shyly they look and leave her where she lies,
And each returns to himself and goes out alone.
In the vacant room the flowers begin to dry.

Late Summer

Alder-side by water fringe, Oriental
With cat-o'-nine-tails, soothed with pads, all
Quick with red-wings, deft with spiders,
Not deep nor dim but drowsed; far with firs.

Clear. Cool. And beyond moss gentle beyond
Fronds of goldenrod, late summer weighted: pond.
Flicker of fish, silver dart over bronze treasure,
Lost and beautiful, abandoned, emptied cans, or
Roots' dark, octopus-vengeful; all image-doubled.
The plains of August august, autumn-troubled.

Seven Lines

Crisscross of hawthorn bush in snow.
Spill of tacks—a thicket—snarled barbed wire: no:
Thorn bush under low ceiling, thrust
Out against wind-troughs of snow-crust:
Unwalked, birdless acres, the air stiff and
Sun gone gray. This diamonded, transfigured dust.
Thorn-thicket: tallest, last thing in this land.

Identities

We cut the grass open,
We dug out the coffin,
We lifted its cover.
After years—nearly twenty—
We let the sun on her.
She lay as we knew her—
In the dress we remembered
And the face of her sleeping—
One moment, then perished.

It lay flat as a portrait
Old, dim beneath cobwebs.

For another's convenience
We caused her removal;
We looked to confirm it—
No mean, ghoulish motive.
But thus did we lose her.
We watched the air smash her,
Her fall from our loving,
Escape from our memory.

O, our multiple errors—
That the dead need move over
To placate the new dead;
That one not of our time
Would sustain introduction;
That we could assume it
And not be changed coldly,
Hurt too by the sunlight

Puzzled and lonesome
We fitted grass over
The new grave and left her
Who, leaving us twice, had
Just now left forever.
It was she had confirmed our
Identifications.

Now That Lost April

Now that lost April returns with the sky
The roads are all dizzied with puddles awry,

The pastures in surf where the bluets are sown;
O the warning my mother would make to me once:
Put something over you when you lie down.

No matter how stilled stands the summery air
The thin threads of east wind shudder somewhere,
Deep in hot daisies cool smell of the ground;
O the warning my mother would make to me once:
Don't fall asleep without some cover on.

Through autumn is slumbrous in umber and high
The forests break open at weight of the sky,
The leaves shred the blood-red, the dry-shaken brown;
O the warning my mother would make to me once:
Have something over you when you lie down.

So in all seasons all lovers beware
Of the cold drill of darkness which spins in the air,
The whisper of spring saying *Winter has come*—
Of the warning my mother would make to me once:
Keep cover over you—keep cover over you—
Keep cover over you when you lie down.

Sixteen Lines

Let fall your gold again
O gold-green maple flowers
Crisscross the morning hours
With your nostalgic rain
Of sun-excited showers
Let fall your gold again
Until the pouring air

156

Drift gold-green everywhere
The sidewalks all along
In all your gold again
Your living carpet wear
Breathe out such sweetness there
Might yet again be song
Peace memory meaningful pain
O gold-green maple flowers
Let fall your gold again

Blue Fish in a Blue Sky

Blue tissue on slat sticks, the kite
Angrily rattles, argues with air,
Springs tensely near overhead in bare
Naked March, in scudding light

As the plunging boy downhill strings
It farther out. It wrestles the wind.
At level peril airways thinned
As water loosed of ice, it rides—it swings

Up in sudden surety—sloughed amateur
Awkward—glides perfect incline.
Now it is a blue fish on his line
Running far in the wind, in its pure

Element high charging, changed, till
Twitch of taut string balks a flight.
Kite sways a-leash at slim height
Above tiny boy braced on the little hill.

He plays-in his beautiful blue fish.
Hooked hard, it bucks stretched cord,
Loops over, rolls wild where it soared,
Diving as though to headlong finish

Leaps side to side. Held it spins
Then streaks down to treacherous trees'
Coral sargasso tangle. But he's
Edging it inch by inch, and wins.

Now clear and close and tamed and tossed
It shudders then slaps flat aground;
Sticks, blue tissue, lifeline wound.
Possessed as meant: almost but not quite lost.

Aria Major

As music well remembered in the mind—
The aria major spiralling secret dusk—
Yet falters on the insufficient voice:
So speak not this, speak not this love.

Wing after wing the fans of evening open
Arching across the sky till massed they stretch
Silent the perfoliated night:
So speak not this, speak not this love.

Wherever underneath midnight you lie,
No longer near enough for me to keep
And soon no longer small enough to hold:
This love, this love, this love I cannot speak.

158

Fifteen Lines

Song sparrow makes a joyful noise
Unto whatever Lord there is
Or, for all of that, to none.
In unpraised flights of praise
Above the pond the swallows play,
They dance a wreathing water and sky,
The choreographers of May.
Honor fitting for this day
Like me they could not know, but they
Are its honor. As a human
In a time of major wars
And minor verse
I would rehearse
Their practice sessions in the sun,
Their encores ignorant of applause.

North Light

Strict invisible wedge untaken,
Immortal interval whose slow increase
Moves with millennial patience;
Dark core in light, shadow of noon
Which defeating us lights us now:
North light: my windows that have no
Sunrise or set save by reflection;
Snow-light; leaf-light; outward, earnest

With chimneys, angled with roof-slant,
Nostalgic with skylights, and slate-stitched.
To island shingle infrequent Crusoes
Climb and repair but never stay:
Invasions unheld, foreignness too great.

North light inward: painters' nonpartisan
X-ray. Here skeletons walk
Being understood, and each thing flames—
Roses, scissors, books and table—
In generation its own sun,
Its joy self-held and emanated,
Its victory shared: individual, whole.
So, too, full-length in mirrors
Stone-naked, 35, the man
Alone between marriages,
Lustrous body entirely stilled.

My desire is for this light only
And long as it may be borne, thereafter
As often; and I know this light is
In me and the room together:
When I am not here the light is not.
Though I stand and stark mirrored
I am abased in its cold pride.
It is earned and given, both; and I
Have made first payments and got
An interest of knowledge, certain now
I work in playgrounds—so this light
May at midnight harden to a star.

A *and* B *and the* Mirror

You there—I here—triangled with the mirror
So it is just your face I see, you mine.
Neither turns to the other, nearer. It is clearer
This way, and at once your eyes begin to shine

And you smile, and I, in quick understood sign
That this is somehow funny and somehow charming,
At first for a moment alarming, then disarming
Not least because it happened without design.

Neither of us speaks—as though this were a magic
Occurrence in whose accustomed logic this un-
Accustomed transference had been done:
Travel has winked and desert plunged pelagic,

And above all we are alone together,
By our shared depth of common light seen clear
Till we laugh for terror, turn, and wonder whether
To dare strength to do it again: I there, you here.

Communication Established

Asleep in the night I dreamed that you owed me a letter
Over and over I dreamed that you owed me a letter.
But when I awoke in the daylight then I remembered
It was other way round, the other way round.

Well, when I was adolescent—in misery mature—
I would dote on the years to come when all must be sure.
Now I see how the green years are greened by their dreams of the
    future—
All the other way round, other way round.

In my art in my century only the old men try singing—
Bare Venus buckled to gray-bearded Mars and clinging.
Those of us yet a-quiver at thigh stand talking
All the way round and around.

I have therefore traveled, my love, to live in our living,
Over and over one green year the time we are living.
For the lechery of lyrics and letters is not lost in loving—
O the other way round

*"We Are So Fond of One Another, Because
    Our Ailments Are the Same"*

There are no girls among us now with small high breasts,
No hard-thighed youth—no man of us golden now.
We have come to this middle island. We are here together.

Across other surfs in seeming other suns we can see them—
The quick-limbed, the nimbus-haired in their reckless and useless
    racing
Bright along the tide edge. If wise we watch without desire.

For we are nakeder than they, in our imperfections, in our being
    together,
Friends and lovers so long, coming through so many waters, so
    many

162

Signs exchanged and discarded, and sharing a few graves and our
     fearful love of children.

To this ripe and middle island, the sun stronger and sweeter since
     we know
How swiftly it can go out. We make love deep and slowly after-
     noons
In the sea sound. We glance back now without bitterness or envy.

Our hands so long have known the shape of each other in the day
     and night,
Change interchangeable, voices and silences easy, solitudes shared.
You nearest—how more than ever tenderly endearing that gray in
     your hair.

Tenants of the House

Beyond this house a rock-jut interrupts
The curve of field: right angle rock shoulder
Sharp and sudden, gray out of the grass:
Incunabulum of skeleton.
Then pond; then pine; and farther west more fields
Crowding a burdock-burdened family graveyard
Rickety slated, faint with fading names.

But there has been no death in this young house.
All earlier houses gone, we live alone
On hungry land in this unseasoned house,
That gray rock a bared bone-thrust of earth,
The slates remindful and the fingering sun.

And now whose dust and bones are those? Can we
Inherit, purchase, hire such ancient death?

But none is alien, uncontinuous,
Though names are signed at last by someone else
And only strangers write them into stone.
We live alone but with the coming child.
That night I dug him, oh I dug his grave.

Memorabilia

Dottle of pipe ash drops dry through the pond water
And the brown pond water sifts it gray down and gone;
Water surface shifts, clears, and shows—amidst halos of alder
Fresh-leafing in May sun—my face, heavy heavy stone.

The phoebe weeps in the woods and the robin chuckles.
Smell of the sun rises out of grass and the rotting bridge;
Beyond me the long sound of falling water. The sky twitches
Small clouds and over my face money-bugs, spiders, midges

Crawl, skate by the dangerous edge. And so I come
To my thirty-seventh season of spring counting so many rings,
Deliberate follies and accidents of wisdom and without fame
Less local than lilacs; though for this rural moment not minding

My face carved out of water, for the real stillness and imagined
    peace.
Not satisfaction. Not contentment. Only the insomniac ambition
Sliding dry through the air as last year's oak leaves
Incidental to mulch. Repeated business of spring is resurrection,

Not distance but renewal, leaf for leaf's sake, new growth green
In its own place by the pond side, twelvemonth repeating its
    variety.

164

Days consume the years but the May day is the waking-dream,
What the morning says to do, the light between the water and the
   sky.

Between one life begotten and one to come, both mine, I have
   come
To this end of winter wish to be taller than I am. Identity is all.
I watch the spiders at my work, spinning the current as they can.
I stand up and walk through the woods and go home to my love.

THE DARK SISTER (1958)

The Dark Sister

I

Across the wide slant of the summer sun
Over the rock-bearing windy meadows of Greenland
Freydis strode like her own shadow, like a woman-shape of night,
Advancing like a queen of darkness, a lean fury
Of flying hair and robes against the thinned gilt of the opened
  west;
She came to the stone house of her half-brother Leif Ericson
And entered quickly like a willful ghost.

The door clanged in the corridor. Freydis called,
"Hello! Where are you, brother? Hello!" hurrying.

  Her husband
Crossed from the great room and Freydis whispered, "Thorvard!
  What are you here for?
I thought I told you to fetch the Norwegian traders. Have you
  been talking to Leif?"

"Leif's in no mood for talk," said Thorvard. "I'd leave him alone."

  "But have you?"

"I've told you. He is out of sorts. Why not let it go? Let it rest a
  few days."

"O Christ that has taught me a new way to swear! Let it go for
  what?
How many years have we got? How many weeks or days?
  How long must I argue this?"

"If Leif hears you now, or if you go angry to him—"

                                        "Don't
  beguile yourself, Thorvard, advising me.

I'm not so helpless, unhelped. Not with Leif Ericson.
    —No, Thorvard: look: you can help me.
The Norwegians are getting restless at our delay.
    I am bound to strike now and settle this.
Take them word that I have come to my brother
    and say I shall meet you all
By the cairn of Eric at dusk-fall and with news.
    Do that for us, Thorvard."

He shrugged thin shoulders as she quickly kissed him.
    "Leave this to me: I know my brother," said Freydis.
"He can talk you tired in his weariness and give
    his doubts such speech you believe them yours.
But if I stay him out and seize his promise
Then we're sure as new axes that they'll cut, as
    good ships that they'll sail. And so we shall.
We'll sail, Thorvard; and we'll cut. You'll see.
    And we'll be richer in this little kingdom
Than all the rest together. Even than Leif."

                             She turned

    away and stopped
On the threshold of the great room; and she stood
With the near-frightened gaiety of an impertinent child
And smiled, head cocked to flirtatious intrusion,
Through a glint-shattered twilight where flanking the
    peat-fired hearth
Leif worked at chess and ale with Tyrker his ancient dwarf.
    Then she laughed,
Flourishing a lean excitement of clattered bracelets,
    flashed rings; and run-to-perch
Upon Leif's chair-arm, Freydis ruffled his gray-gold
    hair and said,
"Tyrker, don't scowl at me so"; and Leif said,
"Go away, Freydis. Whatever you want will keep
    till our game's up"; and moved his king.

Flames hummed on the rock. Through the windowed wall
The regular crumple of waves rolled distanter under
    the dullish cold of white night,
The late light flooding the far fields of the sea.

  "Well,"
Leif sighed, leaning back, "what is it you want, Freydis?"

"An inquisitive raven with secret notions of her own,"
    said Tyrker into his ale.

"For once not a cat? Anyway, never an old and learned owl
Self-throned in an otherwise birdless land."

    "That will do," Leif said.

"Ask her again. For women insistent questioning is
    tribute." Tyrker moved knight to rook.
He jerked with the clumsy nimbleness of the aged
    out of his chair,
Toddled along the hearthstone, his huge head the
    nodding half of him,
Bent hunched-back to the room: Leif's boyhood
    tutor, court jester, wise friend.

"Tyrker, I've a mind to pull your beard." But Freydis laughed
    as she said it.
"Forgive me, both; and by Thor and Loki—who remind
    me of you—
I swear never again to trespass against chess.
    And, darling, don't
Frown like a Christian. If converts are not merry in
    their choice
How shall you persuade the rest to desert the shades
    of Yggdrasil?
—Ah, but I've scratched one bother into another.
    I am indeed a bastard sister. Look:

I'll kiss those angry wrinkles on your forehead as
    though I were that tender wife
You never stayed long enough ashore to get, and now
    are too rich and lazy to."

With an accustomed fortitude, the kind and irritable
    forbearance of a relative,
Of a relieved onetime guardian, of a contented
    bachelor whose evening has been interrupted,
Leif regarded Freydis: from an Icelandic wench who died
    at the birth, his father's by-blow,
Now grown to a smoldering vengeance of greed and beauty
    that having but half
The Greenland royalty of Eric's sons gripped a compellent
    queenliness; and all the more
Since their two brothers were lost on the Vinland
    voyage, leaving Leif alone,
A sailor weary of the sea; explorer of the soul only;
    sure of his last landfall.

With a blandishing dance of her skirts over painted slippers
Freydis whirled on her toes and sat suddenly smiling from
    Tyrker's chair—chin in hand across the chessboard.
"Leif, I must hurry. Those young Norwegian traders,
    Helge and Finboge,
Will come to me tonight with a sea-business.
Before I meet them I need a word of your own to
    meet them with:
A gift of what is abandoned, left, lost, emptied—
    yet yours, and a fief, reclaimed—
A small thing if wasted in the wind, but outpost of
    empire if retaken and lived in—
Your houses in Vinland."

                    "Vinland?" It was not Leif who spoke
But a sad and golden woman in the doorway—Gudrid,
    widow of his brother Thorstein

Drowned off that westward coast seeking their brother
    Thorvold who had got his death there from a native arrow;
Widow again of the trader Thorfinn Karlsefne, worn out
    by the same land—Leif's land.
"Vinland? Who is so mad or rich or reckless
    he'd barter himself for Vinland?"

Snorre, her little son, ran in past Gudrid to Tyrker
    who swung him feebly once around.
"Here," said Tyrker, "is the true heir of Vinland
    —born there—now king in exile.
Have we enough of the treasure-trove left over to
    make him a little wooden crown?
Thorvold lies lost there with a wooden cross, and
    Leif has wooden houses there, empty—
And I see by Freydis' look I have a wooden head.
Come, Snorre; I am eighty and you are four, and
    that makes eighty-four;
So let's be old together and sit on the hearth, and
    I'll teach you the memory game."

Stiff-staring, looking only at Leif, Freydis
Said, "Tyrker's half-memory that is gone seems to
    have held me. As usual.
For Freydis it is always a half—if possible, sort of
    lesser a half, bitter a half, grudged half,
    and even forgotten a half.
Am I an intruder by bastardy? Am I half a woman? Half a
    daughter? Answer me that!
Half by whom? If women are so negligible of themselves,
    why even count me half?
What does it matter whom Eric seized in the dark: a
    woman—or a woman?
How much of you, Leif, is Eric? How much of our brothers
    was he? Yes—yes: Eric's my father, too.
And my father's younger sons—what are they now but
    salt and sand of that Vinland?

The blood is ours and we have signed it red—have
　　paid it out. Now let that land pay me."

Watching her gently, Leif said, "Vinland has paid us.
It has paid us in wounds and many deaths and in money.
You have had all three, Freydis. Enough of each,
　　I should think—even of money.
Lay not treasure up for yourself upon the earth—"

　　"Ah, the Christian gab comes easier
To those who have closed sufficient bargains to be safe
And plenty of breath spared to preach."

"We are safe in God and the true belief—in the heart
　　only, Freydis.
Do not quarrel with me. I do not chide you, but speak for
　　your good.
I doubt if there is more of such good in Vinland."

　　"The wood stands."

"Yes, the wood stands. But we have brought much to this
　　treeless land—
Others more than I. Turned it to gold. It is only
　　a few months
Since your return with Gudrid and Thorfinn, God rest his soul."

"But theirs was the heavy cargo."

　　　　　　　　　　　　"Ah!" cried Gudrid. "Is
　　that what pricks you, Freydis?
But ours was the larger ship and crew. Thorfinn
　　was leader, it was he
Bore the weight of the voyage and our three years' settling.
Surely you and your Thorvard can find no faithless fault."

"This time I lead. And if there's a larger ship and
　　larger crew

Then they'll be mine by right."

"And what," asked Leif, "does Thorvard say to this?"

"He'll say what I say."

Gudrid cried: "I tell you
there is evil in that place.
That land was not meant for us—there is something against us,
Something beneath the soft grass and the bright leaves,
More than threat of savages native there. Some
trick of the sun
Gentles its uttermost kingdom and lures us into it
as if it were
A shining paradise beyond the black cold sea. Those
who go in
Are netted with a silken skein of light, move as
dreamers in dream,
Fancy themselves gods of a sort come miraculously to
an earth-garden of Valhalla
—And are welcomed with poisonous arrows, and yet dream still:
those spared,
Lulled to birdsong and the great shards of the sun
on the coast rock,
The way of the wind in the tall trees, the forested hills
Sighing of peace and wealth and a kind earth
flowering under their feet
—They are sucked weak. I tell you trouble and
danger weave in the air.
Almost I believe again the spinning Norns brood
Watching that foreign thread. It shines bright on the fields,
Yet I think it drags darkly into the ocean and whirls
coldly somewhere out to the sky.
It spins, and they wait. O God, Leif—
Leif, I wish you had never found that land!"

Saying nothing, Freydis looked
With a long, uncomprehending contemptuous stare
    At Gudrid weeping. For a moment there was no sound
        in Leif's room but that sobbing
And the fire hiss on the earth where Tyrker
        and Snorre watched.
Then the little boy ran fearful to his mother's side,
        and she took him away.

Freydis paced the stone floor. Leif studied the fire. The
        dwarf resumed his chair,
Meditating over a castle in flicker of flame-light.
        With thin clashing of braceleted bronze
Freydis clasped and unclasped her strong hands
        as she walked. The fire
Hummed in the rock.

"Leif," said Freydis at last, "you know my mind.
Once it is set it is set. Who shall understand the
        daughter of Eric if not his son?
We inherited stormy hearts. If yours has come to greater
        quietness now
It does not forget its youth and won't refuse mine.
        Gudrid's other stock. Her son, too.
I have no son—nor have I a Leif for a husband—
        let us speak truth.
But marriage freed me of your charity—made me
        an independent woman by law,
And that will do. Thorvard serves me well that much.
        And I am Freydis still.
Don't forget we are whelps of a man driven out
        of Iceland for murder,
Who brought his strength with him and founded this
        edge of the world;

And you sailed farther than that—this was not
    the end, after all.
You are Leif called 'the Lucky.' Yes.
    And I am Freydis, your sister."

"It may be by my coming to a quieter way," Leif answered—
"By the sick smell of our deaths and the taste of
    the sea fouled with them,
I have no longer the old love of the sail and the
    westward wave with sky rising;
Journeys of commerce—these hunts—are not of my kind,
    are a strange child
Born of that innocent voyage:
The new look of the land, with the hawk-prow taking
    the wave-dance—
Wind-shifted sand, sea-drawn, the sun along
    the wilderness edge,
The wild sweet breath of the air coming over the
    great fields: sea-fall, land-lift,
The long light of the summer—old Tyrker, here, drunk
    on the sight of grapes; the ship
Turning home like a purple barge. No; Gudrid speaks false
    out of forgivable sorrow—
Vinland is a good land. I saw it, named it, and we
    have taken a mite of its wealth,
But the land is not ours: we are not enough, we are not
    strong enough for it.
You have felt its angers, seen the unknown, unnumbered
    threat of the Skraelings.
I should myself carry the Cross among them, but a Cross
    with an army;
Even to fetch wood you need not only axes but swords—
    more swords than we have.
Houses?—Any house of mine is yours, Freydis. But on
    those, grass has a better claim."

177

"I have thought it out"—Freydis spoke slowly, carefully—
    "and there is a single way:
The quick voyage."

                "How quick?"

                                "From early fall to late spring."

"When the sun retreats and storms are let loose?
    A rare time to go voyaging."

"Skraelings have never been seen but in midsummer—
    they go south before birds,
Or, for all I know, into holes in the ground; but winter
    is bare of them as trees of their leaves;
We should settle safely, cut wood, and come away."

    "How many of you?"

"Say seventy men divided between the two ships—
    and such women as they have or want.
A quick voyage and a sure profit; the crew from Norway
    is eager; I can match them
With tried sailors willing to go again, and a dozen
    grown boys bold for a venture."

"And the houses—?"

    "Should be sufficient for all. I need the assurance
Of roof and walls without labor—no time lost—
    no hammer and spade, but the ax.
We shall sail home with a rich cargo, and safe."

                                "And then—?"

"And then I shall be content. You'll see me grow a
    dame of home and church,
Lavish in good works, maybe raising sons, sure in my
    fortune, mild by the fireside,

Garrulous as an old Viking over my great days,
    dreaming of time to come
When the men of our race shall increase and sail forth
    to take that land,
Build it and stake it ours."

  Eyebrow cocked to match a dubious smile,
Leif regarded her with skeptic affection pouting his lips,
    tossed a questioning glance
At Tyrker; but Tyrker had folded ale-drowsy into
    his chair. "Well,
Go with God's blessing if go you must, Freydis.
    It is quite an image
You promise to bring me home, and I'd like to see it.
    But I cannot give you my houses."

"But Leif, without them—"

  "Listen to me. If they are there still, you may use them.
But all must be fairly done.
Ax and sword, oar to oar, sail for sail: balance this
    partnership with your Norwegians.
If off you go at an uneven start, sure as you breathe
    you'll wind up hobbling all,
Plain wood turned maggoty under the jealous eying of
    those sore with suspicion of unfairness.
So with my houses. Let them stay mine in name—
    that little of Leif Ericson there—and
You'll be spared onus of envy, be it ever so little. The
    loan of them equally, Freydis—that will do."

Freydis, who while he was speaking had turned away,
    now turned again, facing him
With the light so gone out of her face Leif was
    for a moment baffled,
Thinking she had not heard him or thinking she
    thought he had refused her;

But as he would have spoken her eyes came alive
    again, she smiled past him and
Rushing forward bent over him and kissed him. "Of course
    that will do," she said; whirled, hurried out.

"Monk-heart-searcher Christ hold the hawk-seat,"
    Leif murmured, and the door
Clanged in the corridor, wind thudding in the
    roof-hole; and Tyrker stared awake.

"The dark sister has flown?"

                          "She has," said Leif.

"On her raven's way to your Vinland houses?"
"Yes.

        "I supposed she would. You were never one
    to out-talk that cleft tongue."

"Think twice, old man. I refused her the gift of
    the houses. She's left with a lending."

"That will do."

                    "So she said. So I said. But my name
    is on the houses still, and so on the land.
They are no more hers now than they ever were; and
    no more hers than they are the Norwegians'.
Not that I begrudge her toys which have outgrown me. This
    seemed most just."

                    "And she was pleased?"

"Why—so she seemed to me. Yes, pleased enough.
    Off she's caromed to her business tryst.
She has a plan."

        "Of course. She has them every year like a bird with eggs.

And now she'll hatch them on your boughs, and when they
        roost there
It's liable to be dirty."

                    "I know what you think, Tyrker."

    "If you want to know what I think,
I'll take the prerogative of age and the role of the
        worst of fools—an old fool—
And tell you what I have always thought: Freydis is
        dangerous, Freydis is mad.
Begging the pardon of your father's memory, her mother
        was a hot slut. Eric—
Well, you know he was never a dog suspicious of red meat
        thrown to him.
This is what he got of it, a fevered reckless child.
        All this at the time
He killed the man over land claims, and the lot of us
        sent packing out of Iceland.
He'd nothing but drag this dingy orphan with him, being strong
        —no doubt, to his honor—for the get of his loins.
That's why your mother,
Who died in the faith and, Christ bless her, lived it
        before she'd heard of it,
Brought the girl up as her own. But it was never hers
        and it was never
More than the tag of Eric's pagan past. And how far
        past we may still guess
Since he all but spat upon that priest from Norway and lay
        muttering of Thor his last night.
In any case, there's Freydis. Her mark is the fiery hammer
        of the old gods.
She dreams of power, having been born beside power
        that was not rightfully hers.
If you think there's no harm in that for a woman
        you're a bigger dolt than she

And that is all I'll say, my boy, except that I've
　　checkmated you, and Goodnight."

II

Night stretched a pale gauze of dusk on the land,
The colors of gorse-slope sleeved in a mist of twilight
All gone gray as the rock,
Abrupt mountains
Twinkling with waterfall toward the steep fiords;
Inland the stiff silence of ice,
Shoreward the pulse of the sea, and between them
Moored to the sparse coast the houses of Brattahlid,
Many like Leif's of stone from the time of Eric's founding;
Now many more a weather-silvered wood, cut
　　pine green and oak bronze in Vinland.
The death-light of midsummer midnight
Permitted one star beating low to the ocean, and Freydis
Leaning against the cairn of Eric high on the headland
Turned to regard the three men climbing
　　the hill-road; and called,
"Quickly! I have news—good news!"
And greeted Thorvard and the two Norwegians,
　　Helge and Finboge,
Walking a little toward them, her hand held forth
　　like a man's; she clapped
Her husband's shoulder. "It is done. Leif has given
　　his promise. We have the houses."

"Good," said Helge; "now we can talk."

　Thorvard said, "You are certain, Freydis?"

"No doubt of it: Leif's word is a rock. You know that
　　as well as I. Mine also.
Come, let us sit here at the grave of the king
Who looks forever on the sea which he never crossed.
　　Vinland he left to

Those strong enough to take it. And that's yet to be.
    Perhaps to us."

"And perhaps not," Thorvard murmured, squinting ahead
    at the ocean, his lips
Twisting with an habitual, soft twitch. A small man,
    he sat apart from the other two
That but for the light and dark of their hair bulked
    identical in the twilight:
Solid Norwegian traders, not first of all sailors,
    not the mariners of the old time.
"After all," said Thorvard, "many have looked upon
    Vinland, and some of us housed it;
Yet always we come away—if we are alive."

  "All foolishness," said Freydis; "this fear—
This fear of Vinland is foolish. Anyhow, this time
    we play it the safe way,
So shake no more, Thorvard. Time to come, my friends,
    we shall see.
What others have abandoned, we'll grasp again. The
    claim shall be ours.
Stay with me in this compact, Helge and Finboge, and
    we may yet divide
Half and half the richest province of the world."

  "But your brother Leif?" asked Helge.

"My brother has tired of sea and sail. Hearth, crucifix,
    ale and chess,
Long gabs with that German Tyrker—those are his wants,
    and he fills them,
And money enough to do it. So be it, say I. He's a man,
And what's better than that?"

  "A woman with a plan," Thorvard said, and laughed.
    The others silent

Till Helge said, "Let us all have a plan that will
        work for us all.
What do you say, Thorvard?"

   And Freydis answered, "Share and share alike is easy.
What does your crew number?"

                                        "Thirty men."

                                   "And the women?"

"Perhaps a half-dozen along."

   "Then thirty men it shall be for me," said Freydis,
"And however many other women required. They don't matter.
        Fair enough, Thorvard?
I think"—hurrying on—"yours is the larger ship.
        You have further advantage:
I bring you the loan of Leif's houses
And I know the routes of the sea that will take us there."

"Yet," said Helge, "to go at all you need the men
        that we bring you."

"Oh—no doubt. And in Vinland we shall work the
        wood as a single crew,
Divide alike the cargo we fetch to the Ericsfiord dock.
And—all well—we should be blessed to richness.
You have the quick eye, the ruddy glance of able traders;
I am a simple woman, but born with the salt itch
        of the sea in me.
We should do well together."

"Not at all well apart," Helge said.

"My brother," said Finboge, "is a practical man. Are you
        acquainted with the species? Do you have such
        in your country?

I am his brother but I admire him. I admire him
    but I am his brother; therefore
I see him objectively—not least because he is
    everything that I'm not.
To be sure, we are both bachelors, but there's a difference.
I am practically a bachelor; he is a bachelor—practically.
    Do you see what I mean? He permits no interference
    to serious matters.
His nose for profit is like an owl's for a rat; and rats—
    he'll tell you—were made for the owl's intelligence.
He has a just respect for others only because—he'll
    also tell you—he's a Christian.
I say he's a Christian practically: that is, he will
    mention it six days a week and observe it one.
But that, for all I know, is a good Christian. I've a more
    multiple belief myself, but then I'm the younger.
In fact I do for the most part what he tells me—
    which for once is practical of me.
I'd rather have stayed to home and made up songs and
    gotten nowhere; instead I tag at his heels
—And gladly, gladly. It's the way to see the world:
    with a man who knows it."

"Finboge, Finboge, what a long speech from you!" Helge said,
    laughing and mocking a fist at his brother.
"Pay no attention to him. I'm a simple businessman
    and he dresses me up with his talk.
But I tell you one thing: I play the game fairly.
    Everyone in Norway will say that for me.
I'll take my share but I don't ask more than I earn. A
    chance for everyone—that's my Christian belief
And I find that it's good business. This deal of ours,
    you'll see, will prove as much.

"I have thought," Helge went on, "when we have
    made a good voyage

And come again to Greenland and on with the wood to Iceland
So all may see what a catch there is in the west—
More and more men will be brave and wise enough
    to join in the venture."

Freydis regarded Helge as though to remember and
    interpret him
There in the soft light of the northern night.
    "I'm not so sure.
I can see, Helge, you are a shrewd man; the kind
    who looks so far ahead
He brings in his glance that far-time so much the nearer.
Finboge also, even though he wouldn't say so."

    "Yes," exclaimed Helge with a pitched excitement;
"And we who bet brain, experience and fortune on the
    start of it all
Stand certain to be lords of a great realm; and once
    the native Skraelings are put down
We shall treat them kindly—make of them Christian
    slaves, bring them
Weal of our race. By red shield of war and by white
    shield of peace,
By hawk-beak and by dragon-head of our carved ships,
    and by Christ's rood
We shall build the kingdom of God on the kingdom
    of gold. What do you say?"

"I knew when first I came to you"—Freydis picked her
    words up slowly—
"To try you, if you would follow me in this thing—
    I could see then
You knew the Viking voyage of adventure
    belongs now to skald-song.
Our time is new and changed. Time now to
    strike in, to draw forth.

186

Nor are we longer old traders of inland routes.
　　　See by this summer sun
Circling our mountains like the vast twilight of the old gods
How, too, there is a growing light in the west.
　　　We carry with us
That which we journey towards." She paused, gazing
　　　at Thorvard and Finboge.
"And we have each a silent partner, and all of us
　　　yet another—Leif Ericson.
So that's an honored role. My brother has spoken for us.
　　　What do these two say?"

"I am with you," Finboge said.

　Thorvard's mouth twitched sullenly.
"My wife can speak for me in this. I cannot claim
　　　to be a far-seeing one;
I am not of the house of Eric, but a land trader.
Yet at least I have voyaged the way before and
　　　lived in that land.
Profit I don't despise and I'd welcome more of it.
　　　I say only—
One voyage at a time, and remind you we are readied
　　　at best for a swift run.
We must sail soon to be in harbor too late for Skraelings,
Too early for the fall winds on the western sea.
　　　Ships, men and provisions—
These are our proper business."

　"My hard-headed husband," Freydis said; and they talked
There by Eric's cairn as the air filled slowly
　　　with returning light.

"Will they play fair in the bond?" Thorvard asked
　　　as the Norwegians plodded away to the beach.

her head
That flared in the early wind with the ragged flag
of her black hair,
Freydis hugged her troubled robes and with the
bespelled stare of the blind
Gazed down on the morning ocean as though she
were its born empress
And could have called forth its miles of dazzling
seethe, and the wind-whiten.
Listening, as though it sounded for her alone,
and away across it
Gust of that woodland country, its lakes shining
flat to the sky—
All beyond the ridge of the sea, by westward
and southward drift,
Steering by stars to feel the slow paths of the strange night,
By sun, by snuff of the air to smell landfall;
by bird flight, by watch
Of changing color in the sliding water. "They will
play fair in the bond,"
Freydis said; "never fear. Their sail must follow
ours or never hoist."

Thorvard said, "Helge smarts with his big plans.
And I do not like so many leaders.
The last voyage raveled too much on that."

  "There's no fear of either.
If they've yet to learn how the strong hand is the best hand
I'll teach them. And how one alone is swiftest." She
turned and smiled.
"Once we are in Leif's houses over in Vinland, our
friends the traders
Will be—let us say—our guests. Or—how can they
help it?—hostages of a sort.

They voyage by our cooperation—settle by our
  sufferance—and must follow us home.
They have no choice. They know we are their eyes,
  their brains and their luck.
We could leave the whole lot to be lost, we could turn again
With nothing in our way but their bones. Do you understand?
  There must be nothing in our way.
There's no chalk or lime I wouldn't crush with my
  heel if it fouled our path.
This talk of kingdoms—pretty; pretty enough. And
  such may come. But we by this plunge alone
Can return better at last than second-best. Do you see?
  I'll be reckoned with hereafter.
And there's a sort of crown here.—Yes, they will play fair."

Freydis paused as if she would go on speaking but suddenly
  her eyes flicked sightless, her face death-white.
  Thorvard did not notice.
She said, "Go tell Leif it is settled. I am tired—
  tired. Do not waken me when you come in."

Thorvard alone at the cairn stayed musing awhile:
"Sea that has gnawed so many bones—dog of my old gods—
  I was not born to be hounded by you.
Sometimes I think I wedded a wave of the sea,
  a pulse of the tide,
And am spun like a stick in the undertow—a stick a dog
  might play with but ignores if there's bone.
Certainly salt pours through the line of Eric; but it's
  clotted in some these latter days.
Maybe they are a mighty and famous line, but they die as
  quick as the next; quicker, I sometimes think.
And I know what they think of me: nothing at all.
  I mean: nothing—
Someone they'd never heard of, something Freydis

brought in; and of course to be treated with amiable
    manners since here I am:
'From over Gardar way, wasn't he?' Less than a consort.
    But they'll see. I'll outfloat them all.

"Still, there's Leif Ericson. Sometimes I think he really
    likes me—assumes I am good for Freydis.
Last Yule he put his hand on my shoulder and laughed,
    pleased with my skoal to the family. Patted my arm.
Being much older than I, he's avuncular; kind. O Christ,
    I wish I hadn't knelt in front of him that day
Making that silly obeisance. Foolish in drink.
    I must watch that.
No—he knows I'm no sea-going Viking—I've made no
    bones of it—and himself,
Though he strode the ways of the ocean as no man else, is all
    done with it now. Quieted. No wild man like his father.
We understand each other. I think. I think he respects
    me. A leash upon Freydis.
And the people of Brattahlid treat me everywhere with a
    bow and a scrape. I think they like me better than her.
I think Helge and Finboge do.

"Enough! Enough! This little mouse in my head
Sucking and nibbling: why must I always batter myself?
Perhaps Leif will yet alter his mind as to the
    houses. But I guess not. I'll see him.
This time, maybe, he won't stare at me half a moment
As if trying to remember who I am."

I I I

This Vinland-America, like something the sea dreamed
    between the wind and the light,
Like no land founded; this myth, legend, history—saga
    of the extended sun—

This mirage of meadows reaching out of the western
    immaculate waves,
This new land, unforeseen miraculous child of the earth;
    the wine and the wood—
Lay that summer waiting, while at Ericsfiord the two
    ships were readied and stocked.
And this was one thousand and nine years since the
    Bethlehem birth,
That Eastern light searching from Rome which made on
    Europe a mighty Cross
Glimmering athwart the northern twilight—Götterdämmerung
Long prophesied in the old fables. Blood-wine
    of Christ and Thor's ale mixed,
God-Odin stretched on Yggdrasil, on the Tree of
    the World. This Vinland
Mixed in the shore-sands of its morning-side young Norse bones
Their shrouding flesh fallen, all thinned to ghost,
    haunting their lost graves,
Singing of sweet dew on the printless grass
    under the riding, riding sun;
No odor of man. The fields' wide silence against
    the pines' keening,
And high and foreign the voices of dead Vikings bewildered
    in the wind.
Lost graves and ghosts. Crossness named for Rome's
    sign—the crucifix staked
Where arrow-struck Thorvold was buried—but the
    sticks vanish and the grave;
The name and all the names slide into the surf
    and drift off coast
Moorless and moving—sand-sunken, uncovered again—
    strange—they shine like shields.

At Ericsfiord, downhill from Brattahlid at the sea's edge
    in Greenland, the putting forth.

Gudrid, the boy Snorre, Tyrker and Leif, the folk
    of the village, farmers, old sailors, wives and children
Crowding the russet slopes above the wharf in the
    steep light of noon
Which beat on the water far out, blinding; the sea
    strummed by the sun.
The two prows as the oars rolled lifting into
    the day's soft glaze—
Great open ships low-laden, their high-carved heads
    a hawk and a dragon.
Leif held above his blowing hair that set the breeze
    afire around it
The white shield of peace and luck. "Skoal, Vinland!
    Skoal, Vinland!"
The shouts from the shore sighed over the harbor,
    the sea lobbed louder at ship-side,
Oars' oaken turning creaked a drowsy trouble, sails
    squared to a salt wind
The ships were drawn into the sky.

    Northwest they followed the coast,
Low margin of the land burning still with flowers,
    the mountain-wall craggy,
Hazed with afternoon, the darkening cuts of fiords;
    wind surgent,
Sea traveling easily aft. Freydis, standing near the
    prow of her ship,
Felt the wave beat as though it were the exciting
    pulse of one beloved
And with exalted quiet held it deep within her, not
    speaking. Men at the oars
Glanced at her curiously; the women, whose circle
    she ignored, whispered against her,
They cosseted tales of her lecheries and greeds and
    like their men they feared her.

Graven, Freydis watched the coast-edge thin to a
    slim silver line of dusk
And go out in the thickening night. Air sharpened
    into the sails, twisted
Torch-fire set high on the ship-sterns. So keeping
    sight of each other,
Sea held short between them, oarsmen resting, the ships
Slowed to an idled flowing down the night which
    suddenly filled with stars.
Curve of the course without magnet, chart, or name,
    bent west, but a quick dawn
Showed with clamor of gulls the crescent boats
Hard-in near the coast.
As ocean kindled and shore opened, the day warmed
    on the inland ice
Flashing shield-bright from the blue mountain heights.
The two ships ruddered round reef and island, steering
Between threats of rock. Sun heated the milky
    jade of the waters,
Faded late with a long twilight which on the second
    night deepened to fog.
They crept to a wary searching and soon were trying
    a darkness made
Only of sullen water lost in undiscoverable sky—cold,
    dense blackness, nothing;
That hidden path of the North gods, horror of empty
    night unstarred,
Midnight that out of its silence spawned abrupt ice,
    mountainous, floating.

The drenched torches hissed. The ships were heavy
    with sleepers' breath.
Among the watch tending the beacons on the Norwegians' ship
Were two Greenlanders, old sailors, Erling and
    Thorkel, hired at Ericsfiord

To replace a deserting pair. They had made the
    westward voyage with Thorfinn.

"We were dumb maybe," whispered Erling,
    "coming a voyage like this."

  "How's that?"

        "I don't like the start of it."

"Start of it? Start of it?" Thorkel said "Why, man,
    we've moved as silky as a greased cock to its hot harbor.
Have you lost the feel?"

        "There you have it. There's a time
  for frigging and a time for sleep. And the same for sailing.
You're a sailor as good as me," said Erling, "or thereabouts.
    And whenever did you sail save in the spring?"

"Umm. Once or twice on a short haul perhaps. Or I've
    heard of a voyage or two set in midsummer."

            "Heard
anything good?
Seen 'em come back? No," said Erling, "I'll wager you haven't.
    Spring. Spring is the time to hoist
And home again in the pretty fall of the year before
    the frost's at your knockers
Or savages at 'em as the case may be."

Thorkel said: "Warm your own stones and I'll worry for mine.
    There's a plan here; haven't you heard?
Skraelings have weather too, the same as ourselves;
    and the other hangings you mention.
It was early on in the summer we saw the buggers,
    and bare-assed as your face—though I mean nothing else—
Never in the chill or the cold of the early spring. They've
    a place, I tell you, where a stitchless man's at ease;

194

Or a stitchless heathen, anyhow. Or, all I know, they
    burrow into the ground as dead as a bear.
So: we arrive in the dust of their heels and sail home
    again before ever they're awake and around—
And some, so I hear, so weighted with wood even the
    lowest of the crew—say yourself for example—
Will, thank you, be stinking with money."

"It's an easy song as you sing it," said Erling, "but
    I still say it ain't natural."

"How many years have I known you? In how many ships, Erling?
    And, by the jumping gods, you've fretted 'em all.
Meanwhile, my little old sailor, here you sail."

    "And who was it," said Erling, "talked me into it?"

"Ah, you're at me again, you sucker," said Thorkel. "I
    didn't drag you along. The shine of Norwegian wages
Dazzled your eyes, and you know it."

                      "The more fool me," said
    Erling: "sail under foreigners the wrong time of the year."

"Sing it. Sing your own song—and to yourself. I'm
    tired of the refrain.
At least we're not under the bitch on that other ship."

"Nor over her, either."

    "And for that you can thank all the gods you please.
Still, I don't know," said Thorkel; "I hear it's been done.
    And not only by Thorvard. You remember
Thorhall the Hunter, on Thorfinn's voyage, that black-shagged
    giant of a man? You remember him?
If that spike didn't nail her, I'm a slippery diddler; which,"
    he added, "I'm not. I've a small man's compensation."

"So," said Erling, "I've seen. And perhaps her twitch
    of a husband has similar talent.
We're safer, I guess, with Norwegians."

  "So long," said Thorkel, "as they stay safe with
    Freydis. Helge's a man."

"That Finboge listens better, thinks more, and says less.
    He don't give an order easy, but I like him.
He seems such a younger pup. Ah, well," ended Erling,
    "there's a smutch of light in the sky.
I've a stream for over the side. Then we wake the others
    and get some Norwegian-guarded sleep.
Much good may it do us."

                    "Valkyria," Finboge said, the
    torch-light
Shuddering on his young face, the fog blowing steady
    in the night, as suddenly he stood behind them.
"Maybe we are not so guarded, but we are led—we are chosen.
    Yet even you Greenlanders don't know.
Have you forgotten Odin's heaven so soon?
Oh, yes: we give our little orders and take our little
    orders—by the way: thank you—
Pull oars—slack rope—run errands—eat—drink—sleep—
    now and then pee on the sun or the stars in the sea,
Forgetting—not knowing—all the time we are chosen—
    are led.
That woman has fire to breathe. Valhalla sends
    proof before us.
Come—come: you are sleepy. You have overstayed
    your watch with your gabbing.
Go wake the others and I shall rouse Helge.
    Morning's a long way off."

"He talks of demons, doesn't he?" whispered Erling.

  "Well he may," said Thorkel. "Norwegians are an odd lot."

Clearing. Sea steady for days.
Sea bright and the air hot. Wetted hulls
Riding, riding up the way west.
Sky. Sea. Sky. Sea.

At night
New stars made a strange anonymity of heaven, but at last
Thinning darkness showed low in the sky a blue coast
Lying like a long cloud at the sea's end. From Freydis' ship
High in the prow a hunter's horn exultant, and glad cries
Shouted across the morning waters; all crowded and stared,
      and all that day the two ships
Came down toward the far shore as it grew taller
      into the air, and brown and gray
With great rocks slabbed straight out of the ocean; and soon
Cold crash of waves at the stone base of that treeless land.
      Helluland.
Drawn near each other, they stood offshore for the night.
      This was Helge's wish,
Opposed by Freydis who said, "There is nothing here
      but rock—I have heard Leif tell it.
The day wasted on it is one less day for trees.
      What do you think you came for?"
But among the crews excitement of land was too heady
      and Freydis gave in,
Grumbling to Thorvard, "There are rocks enough in Greenland.
      Why didn't they stay there?"
And sulked unspeaking all day. A side-boat with men
      from both ships
Made land through a coastal crevice. They returned
      with tales of wastes
And with killed foxes that had gazed at the Norse arrows.

   Cheered by the feast,
Freydis called to Helge's ship, "Make ready to get
      under way and follow.

Night will stay clear, and from now on we'll have land
    along the voyage."
They traveled now without fear. The evening coast-breeze
    gentled the sails,
Tidal waters clubbed the bows under the oars' sweeping,
    and a new day
Shone upon land flat, forested in the sun,
    bright-edged with beaches,
The dark towering hush of the primordial woods
    above them broken only
By sudden wings out of the hemlock, foreign cry of
    birds or animals' echoed barking.
This shore was Markland, the wind off it fragrant of leaves;
In level early sun the high silhouettes of the
    carven ships—hawk and dragon—
Gliding like soundless ghosts of myth, shadows on the shore. The
    noon sea
Glassed deeply shuttling gardens of fish. Lines went
    out over side. Catch was easy. They ate well.
Some of Helge's men put in at an island and killed bear,
    but almost without pause
The two ships silently, steadily rowed south: the soft
    sliding of the hulls
Moving along the stillness of the land.

                        A sailor's voice singing:

    "I saw there wading through rivers wild
    Treacherous men and murderers too,
    And workers of ill with wives of men;
    There Nithog sucked the blood of the slain,
    And the wolf tore men; would you yet know more?

    "Brothers shall fight and fell each other,
    And sisters' sons shall kinship stain;
    Hard is it on earth, with mighty whoredom;
    Ax-time, sword-time, shields are sundered,

Wind-time, wolf-time, ere the world falls;
Nor ever shall men each other spare."

Fold and fold the quiet of land and the traveling waters;
    a night and a day
The ships descended the great cape of Wonderstrand;
    the piled sand's
Hairy skyline of rolling dunes, cloud-rounded and bright.
Leif had named it because of the long sailing.
They groped into little coves and away. In one a keel
Jutted salt-crystal-crusted out of beach wrack:
Vertebrae of the longboat Thorvold sailed the
    summer of his death.
Crossness.

  "Here I shall go ashore," said Freydis. "I want no
    one with me.
Let the longboat stand by till I call.
    Give me your sword, Thorvard.
Skraelings I don't expect, but they may expect me."
    She laughed. "You can go fishing."

And set ashore near the skeletal hull she strode
    past it, the sword a staff,
Into the high dunes plodding a slow track till they
    towered about her; glassy hills,
The sharp green beach-grass wind-shined, hiss of the
    blowing sand, the sea muffled.
Chilled in sullen shadow—that flew and returned—
    Freydis pulled her dark red cloak closer
And sat by a scrub bush gazing around the vast bowl
    of the dunes. Idly, both hands on the hilt,
She pushed the sword-point in and out of the sand.
    She said aloud:
"Thorvold?

        "Wherever your near grave is hidden, hear me.
    I see you there.

Stilled, all but that golden hair that Eric gave to his sons but
    not to me.
I see it brighter even than these sands. But the sands
    cover it over,
Cover the arrow the Skraelings drove in your heart,
The cross those Viking Christians stuck at your head,
    both lost with you, lost.
Dark. Broken. The grave shifting deeper. But I
    see the hair shining.
You hadn't the luck that goes with it. Nor Thorstein,
    either—but he married soft trash.
The luck was all for Leif.

  "I married soft trash, too, but it has a coin clink.
And for women it's not the same. My first night left me
    hard. And that was good.
Now I can take what I like or leave it. If that's not
    joy for a woman,
Then maybe it's better than joy. Look at the happy
    housewives. They make me sick.

"You know how it always was: you and Thorstein were
    Eric's sons, but neither was first:
No, you became a famouser, lesser thing: Leif's
    younger brothers. And so?
Yourself followed Leif's westward path—a sage imitation,
    except you got killed;
And Thorstein set sail to be a big man too, but he
    tumbled into the sea.
We had always known: Leif was the one.

  "At least you were men. Think of me:
Born offside the line. Breasted and slit.—Ah, what a wife
I'd been for Leif Ericson! One man—one real man
    among us. But no,

I was too near him for that—a ward, a dependent,
    a semi-sister. Rubbish!
I wonder if ever he thought of it. Well, he has your
    deaths and the folly of the Cross,
And gray in his golden hair. And I am free
    to go my darker way.

"The difference—the nearness with the difference—
    that may be everything, Thorvold.
This black hair. These vacant thighs. Who should take
    in Vinland if not I?
What Leif had named and blessed—but left alone—
    it would not accept quick boys.
But I am here, and the blood-right is mine.
All is sexed otherwise. But the pulse is Eric's and
    the sword is in my hands.

"Those others. Let them help awhile but they
    cannot hold. I know that breed:
Gudrid's Thorfinn and all that uncertain crew—clever clay,
    not the old rock. They mold easy—don't stand long.
These are the same rubble. Mix in a little of the gold
    they love, and they crumble.
Finboge's a younger brother and hides a secret or two—
    you'd know him at once.
I can have him secrets and all when I want him.
    Helge's a blunt blade.
He's the kind who thinks any man is wiser than any
    woman. We'll see. We'll see."

For a moment unspeaking, Freydis stared at the
    sword before her.
It shone broad and cold in the shadow-filled dunes.
    She moved it idly in the sand,
Then slowly traced her name FREYDIS; stood and
    rubbed it out with her foot.

"I'll dig deeper than that," she said aloud. And
        dragging the sword through the dusk
She climbed the sliding hills toward the sea and the ships.
"Farewell, Thorvold!"

Into cold rain, islands to larboard, they sailed south:
Straum, a circle of bluff-cut mass coraled with
        eggs; gulls mewing
Wild and white in the storm; and southwest along the
        mainland—past Straumfiord,
Where Thorfinn and Gudrid had built their huts among
        grain and grape; they coasted
With light sail under continuing rain a second day;
        the course swerved
West by rough of rock-shelved headland black in the
        mist; by nightfall,
The flying rain sharp on their backs, rowed north among
        islands in a great bay—a fiord
Like an inland sea flooding. The rain slacked and failed and
        the early morning
Cleared through a steam of fog, dragon and hawk-head
        arching into the sun.
They moved silently, feeling a slow way up the glittering
        day. Tide poured past the bows.
At either hand the sandy shores rose into easy meadows into
        timbered hills.
Gulls wreathing, wreathing over the waters, and a mesh
        of birdsong out of the fields,
Sweet fragrance of land warmed on the east wind
        crossing the ships.
They moved toward Leif's place, toward Hop, the air
        quieting; still; the land around them
Like something the sea dreamed, the land
Between the wind and the light, carved out of glacial rock;

202

Like something secret the sun nourished; like no land
    man-founded,
Rising in stone-bright shores, in beaches slung below
    green bluffs, beyond in-running waves,
Shining fronded and richly weeded, firred, and over
    immaculate meadows that widened and burned
All the way to the woodside:
Birch among beech against oak into pine and the
    wind-flood through them always
Like a land-tide, a golden surf shoulder-deep
    like a noon ocean,
Like something the sea begot when the sea was scoured
    by light and earth made,
Earth lifted to winey-wood as the waters fell
    withdrawing, withering
From flowering of land between the wind and the light;
This latest land; this newest earth—strident in
    the causeways of the west.

And the two ships slowed to their entrance—Freydis'
    leading but Helge's almost alongside—
An inlet. Three longboat lengths offshore, keels
    slodged and stopped,
Helge's was first moored, and many of the crew went
    overside—shouting, swimming, wading
They flocked to the land; others and the women sculling
    quickly after.
Flush-faced, Freydis cried, "We shall do this orderly,
    one boat at a time;
We are not drunken scavengers."

    The Norwegians hastened uphill toward the houses
Weathered, low-pitched in the tall grass; Finboge
    running with the men;
Helge stood stolid on the beach, watching the
    Greenlanders disembark.

Without speaking, Freydis walked hurriedly past him,
Leaving Thorvard. She pushed through the throng standing
    uncertain before the row of houses
And entered the sagged-open door of the largest, known to be
    Leif's own, the one where she had lived before.
Now all were ashore, milling about in the meadow,
    awaiting direction.

"You like it here?" Freydis asked, finding Finboge in
    the dun gloam of the room.

"I do. It is a strange, soft country. Unlike any other."

    "I thought you would.
It is far from home. Here we make our own rules, if any.
    And our own altars.
This is my house." She paused, regarding him with a
    curious look of expectation.
"Though it's not soft, really," she said. "But I know
    what you mean. It's like a woman";
And smiled.

    Blocking the thin late light in the
        doorway—so that Freydis turned—
Helge said, "Why have you deceived me, Freydis?"

                                        "What do

    you say?"

"You have deceived me. We agreed, did we not, on thirty
    men for each ship?"

                    "Well?"

"I have counted thirty-five out of yours—besides Thorvard.
    That was not the bargain."

"You are mistaken."

204

Helge watched her with a persistent, puzzled patience:
"No. I made certain of thirty-five. Thorvard has
    just now admitted the number.
We agreed on thirty, Freydis."

Her eyes flaming, she looked from one brother to the other.
"Where is the fool?

                    "Do you dare question what I do?
If it weren't for me you'd not be here at all, nor
    your fortune certain.
Men have come in search of these shores and died
    here; others have sailed here
And turned away again once and forever.
This country has a friendly face but its tricks
    baffle even the strong,
They turn away, safer elsewhere.
Remember who I am. Remember I came before—suffered
    the dangers of war and weather,
And sailed home secure, yet have turned again
Into the threatened path: the first to go by deliberate
    will twice to Vinland.
You are here because I have led you here. And the
    wood is here. Do I get no thanks?
Must you begin by quarreling with me before our shoes
    are dry from the tide-rim?
Is this your bargain—the moment you are set ashore
    you oppose me?"

In a striding fury, her voice shrill above the clashing
    of her bronze bracelets,
Her hands clutched, thrown wide, beating—in a
    fear-fed anger that frightened
Finboge and balked Helge to amazed alarm—her voice
    clear to the perturbed crowd outside,

205

She cried, "What little even-up of numbers could
     balance, my bargaining friends,
The weight of my service to you? You are not sailors
     but traders. You should know
A good thing when you see it. Well, I think you did.
     Why haggle a tiny difference?"

"Come, Helge," said Finboge, plucking his brother's
     sleeve; "let us not argue.
It is, as she says, a small difference."

  But Helge stayed as though locked. Thorvard came in.
Still walking back and forth, Freydis ignored him.
     But he said,
"We shall not thrive if we have trouble—and that is
     the main thing. Let us be friends.
This numbering of crews is no matter. No harm was
     meant. It was only
At the last moment at Ericsfiord a few more, eager to
     sail when they saw the look of success,
Begged us to sign them on. We thought nothing of it."

  "So did many come to me," said Helge,
His voice edged sharper. "And I had the space but we
     had the bond. So I supposed.
Except for Erling and Thorkel who replaced two men of
     my own, I sent them off.
Two or three, I think, I see now among your crew.
     Surely they would have told you?"

"I do not gossip with sailors," said Freydis. "Nor hire
     those preferring another master.
No. I looked for strong arms and shoulders, made to
     turn an oar and swing an ax.
If we set a number—well, I intended an approximate.
     You'd the same chance as I."

206

Pale, his mouth working with quickened twitch,
    Thorvard said, "Let's forget it.
Finboge, I'm certain, already agrees with me.
    Had you spoken, Helge,
We'd have redressed the balance. It's a small
    matter. No harm done.
You and Finboge with your men make thirty-two,
    and we thirty-six."

"Not counting me," Freydis snapped. And then she
    laughed shortly. "I hope, Helge,
You are not counting me as a man? Thorvard can tell
    you different. Even Finboge
Counts me a woman, I'm sure. Don't you, Finboge?

  "Come now," she said in the pause,
"I do not wish for angry blood between us.
    We've greater bother
Than a man or two one side or the other. My brother Leif
Lent these houses to me, and now we are here and I see
    how few are stout
I fear I must maintain proper claim upon them."

                              "But, Freydis—"

"Be still, Thorvard. Leif is my brother. In this
    I alone have the right to speak.
In Greenland, I know, we made talk—some talk
    of sharing. But let it go."

"You mean," asked Helge, "we must build houses of our own?"

"You others; yes."

  "But, Freydis, I know your brother. This is not his way."

"Helge, I'm in no need of words from you or any
    man concerning Leif Ericson.

My wishes are his always; and he would agree in this.
    How did we come here?"

"Just so," said Helge. "You set the whole voyage
    by Leif's word on his houses."

"His word to me."

        "But—"

    "But—but. Do not try me further in this, Helge.
I have brought you here as surely as though you
    were blind. Can't you understand that?
Can't you be grateful and let small things stay small?
    Why do you oppose my every turn?
I tell you, you'll have me out of temper again; and
    I shan't so easily give in.
How much sharing do you need to make you content?
    Things do not
Turn out always the way we hope. And that's all
    that's happened.
I have—it is true—a few more men than I first
    thought. They need a bed and a roof.
There are strange women among your lot—better they
    stay out of arm's reach.
I want trouble no more than you. You can build quickly enough.
    These houses are mine."

To the still and darkening room no sound came but
    the siege of cicadas
High in the near trees. Then Helge said, "I fear
    this is evil, Freydis;
But we want no trouble. We cannot strive against you."
    And the brothers went out.
They gathered their people—curious, anxious—and
    walked away between the weathered huts

208

To a place hard by the wood's edge and farther up from
    the sea. Helge talking.

In the room Freydis said to Thorvard, "Come with me,"
    and she went out to their crew:
"The Norwegians," she said, "insist that Leif's houses
    are too few and too old for them.
They will build their own encampment. If they
    desire new houses,
No harm in that. And we shall have greater space
    and comfort and sooner get to our work.
Thorvard and I will live here in Leif's house.
    Gather around and my husband
Will make the other allotments."

    Southeast out of earshot, the Norwegians
Clumsily blundered about as though to find the feel
    of the land in the twilight;
Helge stern and encouraging; Finboge silent;
And then they returned to their ship for the night.
    Torch-fire shook on the water;
Uphill, the tall red campfires.

IV

"Monk-heart-searcher Christ hold the hawk-seat,"
    said Thorvard in the morning.

"They will build well enough," said Freydis, "without
    your watching from afar.
Helge harries them to a hurry—you can see from here.
    Even the women. They'll not be long.
You'd better be back in the woods with an eye to our
    own men's axes.
Why, I don't know, but when you borrow Leif's words
    they go spit-slick in your mouth.

Well, you're no Ericson, are you, Thorvard? No matter
    how hard you try."

In the bright and blowing quiet of cool day, the work
    of ax-blade against tree-trunk
Knocked and knocked along the wind.

    "I meant only," said Thorvard,
"A hope for good will among us. Leif's words would be
    Leif's wish. Mine also.
Good will means good trade."

    "Make the sign of the Cross over it if you like,
But a stout hand to manage the blessing does no harm
    either," Freydis replied.
"They are enough advantaged without your prayers.
    And I smell trouble.
Helge swells with ambition, and Finboge makes
    him a proud shadow."

"Yet we have irked them, Freydis."

    "Quite as I wished. It is well with such people
To show the fist first. Even dogs understand it.
    And that is all I have wished."

"No doubt you are right. But let us never flourish it so
    strongly as to menace ourselves."

"That I'll take care of. You watch the Norwegians work,
    hear what they say—be eyes and ears—
Be the leaves on the trees around them, be the
    grass underneath their feet.
Victory crows or snarls—how I long for that
    voice!—but plotting ambition whispers.
Learn to interpret breathing—hear blood in a sigh—
    see knives in a soft look.

210

Do that, Thorvard. Be everywhere. And be a whip
    on the backs of our own men—"
And, as she watched him disappear into the
    woodside: "And be out of my way."

At the far end of the cleared field, cutting and fitting timber,
The Norwegians built rude sheds.

                             Helge said to his brother,
"Beware of that woman Freydis. She eyes you with
    a speculative eye.
She's not the first dark bitch to be teased by the
    sight of a blond head,
And she'd swallow you up as night swallows day."

    Finboge said, "There's Thorvard."

"You are even younger than I thought. 'There's
    Thorvard.' Can't you see it isn't so?
He isn't there at all. Yes: you are young enough—you are
    ripe enough. Freydis sees that.
And Thorvard's no more my objection than he would be
    Freydis'. The woman has claws and fangs.
She's not to be played with."

    "I see you think me stupid, Helge; and so does she.
But I know what her eyes mean—and her white arms
    coiled with all that bronze,
The sharp way her hands lift to her deep bodice. But
    now she is angered with us.
It is most dangerous, is it not? She frightens women
    and makes all men uneasy.
And even frightens men."

    "I am not among them," Helge said. "We have done
    nothing unfair;
The offense and faithlessness have all been hers. Even
    unprovoked she rants madly.

Which I don't understand. We are venturers in this all
    together. She reasoned that clearly enough.
Now it is as though she were wrapped in a sea-change
    and having returned to Vinland
Stalks about like an empress alone above slaves."

  Flushing, Finboge said,
"If you are right—if it is true she looks on me with
    a kinder eye than on most—
Can we not use that to our profit? Should I not—
    I mean—at least go to her,
Entreat her friendship—flatter her with—well,
    with words—and—"

                 And Helge laughed,
Cuffing his brother's thick shoulder. "Finboge, you
    are a good boy and you mean well,
And I guess she'd have wordless use for you in the
    night. But as an emissary,
No more use than I. Traders are not ambassadors
    nor fighters; both roles
Require too much love of something else than money.
    And don't forget it."

"But we must strive somehow to get on in peace,"
    Finboge said. "Not to, is mad."

"Let her have her houses," Helge soberly said. "They
    may be the throne she wants.
Like Leif himself, these Greenlanders are Christian
    now. We should work together:
In that there is much healing; and as for the shares
    of the wood, our ship's the larger.
Whatever Freydis' crew may number she'll carry so much
    and no more; we are freed now
Of any hair-splitting half and half: the woman has
    talked us all out of that.

And when in the spring the lumber sails the sweet
    odor of this land over the sea,
Ours will be heavy—heavy. Come, now—"

Ax-time.
The cut of iron thudding deeper into the forest,
North and south the clearing looped further inland
    like a traveling tide,
Day in, day out, opening the land and the sky.
Tearing plunge of the trees earthward: small logs piled
    by the houses for winter fuel,
Long timber trimmed and heaped at the shore for the
    spring voyage.
By Freydis' demand, the two crews labored apart, and
    each day she walked the beach-rim,
Judging the separate stacks of logs; sharp and short
    in her speech with Thorvard,
Saying little to anyone; much alone.
To the women, weaving and mending cloth, busy at the
    fires, she said nothing—never joined them;
She muttered to Thorvard of whoring among the Norwegians
    whose womenfolk lived in a hut together:
"A loose lot of foreigners," she said, ignoring such
    stealth as rustled at night upon shared beds in her own camp.

Wind-time.
Noon burned through a smoky haze under a glazed sky,
    but the sun going soon,
Night glittered with harder shine, and morning
Frosted with visible breath as the men dug deep pits
    in the clear sand at high tide,
Trapping halibut, sacred fish, where the waves withdrew.
Each day they hunted wild fowl, deer, bear, in the woods;
And the knock of axes, trunk after trunk.

Scarlet now were the flanks of the forest, the yellow
    flakes of the beech trees drifting
Like tossed and driven butterflies across the pines'
    black wall; and Freydis,
Coming upon Helge as he bossed the lugging of lumber
    down to the shore, said,
"Good timber you have there."

    Surprised, after her weeks of silence, Helge answered,
"Yes. You have led us to a miraculous country,
    Freydis. The gold of these leaves
Stripped and strewn on the ground bares what will
    turn at home to a hardier gold."

Freydis neither answered his smile nor looked at him.
    She said, staring at the hauled logs,
"I think you are getting the best timber."

    "But, Freydis, we cut this end of the forest to please you.
Whether this wood is better or worse or different
    at all I do not know.
We have cut where you wished us to and have not complained."

    "How can I be sure, Helge,
That your men do not steal in the night, dragging logs
    from my lot to yours?"

Angered, Helge said, "You can post a guard and be sure."
    And then with a sigh:
"Oh, Freydis, you wrangle your own distrust, nothing
    else. Is there no way
For peace among us?"

                But Freydis turned darkly away,
And darkest among the chilling shadows of the late
    afternoon, followed the field-edge—
The grass leaf-choked and red-vine-tough among rock
    and stump, the air overhead

Cracking with ravens' cumbrous and crying flight and
    the rattling seethe of the wind—
And finding Thorvard she said, "The Norwegians, I think,
    are better paid and sterner ordered.
You must push ours harder or these brothers will
    sail with the richer load.
I have talked with Helge—taken his usual abuse;
    —I can see he's not
Anxious for equal sharing. He has the look of a man
    doing well for himself."

"Trust me," said Thorvard. "A word here and there
    of envious-seeming concern
May have made them think they are taking the richest prizes,
I have learned to look dubious and to murmur, and so
    they have learned a loud confidence.
Now what do you say to that?"

  "Why, Thorvard!" Freydis said, smiling.
  "I say: 'Why, Thorvard!' "

Evening spun its disks of cold—pools of tenser air
    circling out of the valleys,
Enormous moon stilling the land,
Fragrance of wood-fires coiling the night,
Of the wine-making,
Of the resinous trees,
The great salt bay lisping the gray beaches at the
    full tide of the year.
Ax-time. Wind rising.

                    Snow falling.
No one knew when the snow began, so soft in the night
    the snow began
Walking the world. Its lines thickened and hissed in
    the woods, wandered upon the waters; it swirled

Dancing over the fields. The encampments woke to field,
    sky, sea gone, only the snow
Falling and filling enchanted country with deeper
    silence. All that day.
By nightfall on a change of wind the snow lashed
    level from north,
Whipped writhing the forest, shrieked over the crash
    and rumble of the sea;
The Norse huts on the land between trembled, but they
    were nearly hidden—dark caves
Under the steep snow.
                          Till the second noon burned
        through last spent flakes
And from the immaculate drifts of the world to the
    wide washed sky the air
Shimmered with tall dazzles of flame. Running at
    the snow-rimmed shore
The surfed blue sea burst its repetitive snows and
    towering before it
The rounded stacks of timber were like white cairns.

   Hooded and furred, dwarfed darkly
In the new world, by twos and threes the Norse began to
    work ways out, cut paths to woodpiles,
Called across deep acres. Roof holes erect with smoke.
    Shared danger of weather
Joined the camps; and when the men dug through, Freydis
    said nothing.

   A gradual increasing excited coming and going—a merry
Babbling; defiant a little, and never knotted too
    near the house where Freydis watched;
Quieted all at once when suddenly she appeared and
    strode toward them,
Her red robe round her but her black hair uncovered
    to the graying afternoon.

216

"There'll be no work in the woods for a while now,"
    she said. "You'll be glad of that.
Well"—and she smiled with proud beneficence on them—
    "let us be glad together.
The time for the celebration of Yule season is near.
    I'm no wizard of time
But my bones feel the year's end and my blood feels
    the need of wine.
Would that be to your liking?"

    Surprised to relief, Greenlanders and Norwegians alike,
Grinning with gratitude of children who find forgiveness,
All shuffled and murmured. Finboge cried out, "A skoal
    for Freydis!"—his eyes happy;
And was raggedly echoed by other embarrassed voices.

    "Very well," she said.
"Let us take two days to make ready. You men must hunt
    for a great feast.
We women will clear a wide place in front of my house
    and floor it with green boughs;
Forest and sea will be the walls of our Yule temple,
    and spangled sky its roof.
Wine in the ale-cups, kettles and fires: we women
    will prepare all.
Let everyone dress in his best and all gather
    on the third night."

    The third night star-stilled
Bloomed with the massive fires which ringed a
    vast room of flame.
Black, black beyond it the silent, the lost depths
    of continental night,
And the far, high heaven over the climbing thunder
    of fire; and center

Amidst strewn heaps of slaughtered deer, the clumsy
    mound of a bear, piled fish and fowl,
Cauldrons boiling; copper bowls dark-glistening with
    gathered blood, and everywhere
A turbulence of people. A minotaur meeting: the men
    in their horned helmets
Crossing back and forth against the light—busy
    with knives at the carcasses.
Tall in their softest cloaks the women passed the
    wine-filled consecrated cups.
Fortune enjoyed and luck to come were poured to
    shouting laughter; heat of the fires
Warmed them to sweating gaiety; night itself simmered
    with fragrance of food and wine,
Sharp evergreen trodden, nostalgic wood-smoke—other
    Yules and years and countries.

"Men of the sea!"—Helge, brave on a rock, his
    spilling horn held high—
"Men of the sea who have dipped oar in nameless
    waters to Vinland shores!
Women of the hearth, home-keepers, keepers of fire
    even at the wilderness edge!
We have endured the changes of the sun; cut wood;
    hunted the field; fished the ocean.
Again we begin Thor's month in the name of God,
    the Christ God,
On this Yule eve of his birthday. Let the sign of
    the Cross bless all here!
Let the sign of the Cross bless Vinland and our
    treasure in this earth!"
And with ancient horn of Norse myth, old trumpet
    of Asgard, Valhalla's voice,
Helge made the Roman sign in the livid air, his hand
    wine-bloodied. "Skoal!"

The roars rolled over the night. The men touched the
    flanks of the bear for luck,
Ancestors' habit. Now in the new land it was not the
    new god nearest them
But the riding gods of their cradles. Yggdrasil on which
    Odin hung, Tree of the World,
Mighty-branched father of forests, massive ash, and
    growing between heaven and hell,
No man lost from its shade—even here, they dreamed, even here.

    Revelry
Twirled the long night and a day and a second night.
    The drunken slept and rose again;
Tirelessly festival went on, a feasting and fornication;
    none merrier than Freydis,
Gay among songs and old stories, hearty at meat and wine,
    a flirtatious lady
Eluding strange arms and Thorvard's, yet gracious
    amidst the permitted passions,
And even far into the second night.

    Finboge found her pacing the mild darkness beyond the fires.
"This air," she said, "gentles from east. Omen of a short winter,
    perhaps.
Do you think so?

                    "Why do you stand there and stare at me so?"
"Because you are a goddess, a Valkyria walking
    the world. Has no man
Ever said that to you?"

    "Had I heard so pretty a speech before, I should remember."
She smiled and stepped very near him and looked
    straight into his eyes, level with hers.
"But are you sure it's a man speaking it now and not—
    well, shall we say, wine?"

"Ah, you make fun of me. You think me a fool of a boy."

"I thought merely
Valkyrias were not a custom any more."

"No—no, you do not think that," he said.
"Wine lets me say only what I've said a long while in my heart.
You move like a queen of Asgard among us. You despise
    us all—me most of all—
And why should you not, for you are a queen of Asgard.
    You are wise, beautiful, brave.
You scorn us, use us as you will, do as you like.
    You are not in Christ's account."

Freydis watched him with a curious stare. "I will say,"
    she said slowly,
Drawing her finger down his cheek, "I will say that
    the liquor of the Christian Yule
Gurgles in you like a pagan."

"And why should it not? Does one of all this crowd
Believe the Roman riddle? Do you?"

"Many, I think, believe and are pious Christians."

"Our childhood gods are mighty gods."

                              "Even in their death?"

"They live. They wander still
In the skull of the sky. Can you not feel them
    here, closer than ever? This land
Nearer the courts of our kings?"

"It is a strange land, Finboge; I agree."

"No, it is not strange. Here we are nearer. I feel
    the ravens of Odin in the night.
The feet of Freya riding with fortune these northern
    causeways; the tub of the wind

Thunders with sea's lashings down the hidden paths,
    and there is the Norn silence
Weaving and watching and whispering when we should
    sleep; and nearer
The sound of the drums of doom. We have come so far
    we stand close to the skull the dwarfs uphold.
These trees—these thousand thousand trees—what are
    they but Yggdrasil twigs!
We cut and we cut but there is no end. And this Yule feast—
How the gods must smile on its familiar riot to
    the tune of a new name!"

"I have heard many tales," said Freydis, "of your
    Christian King Olaf and his priests.
The sword of Odin and hammer of Thor have jumped
    often in Christ's name.
The word of Rome has a fist and sting—so they tell me.
    Let the King of Norway scourge whom he will
So long as it be for heaven's cause. King Olaf is very
    fierce for God—so Helge tells me.
It is a new way of love, they all say."

    "Ah, you do not believe these ways, Freydis."

"What I believe and what I don't believe need never
    worry heaven or any man.
I believe in Freydis as a mortal woman. And warm.
    Touch me here and here and see."

"Freydis!"

    "Yes. Whatever you are right about, you are
    wrong in one thing: I don't despise you.
Come, Finboge. Come with me."

    —"Or do I despise all men?" said Freydis aloud,
    walking homeward alone

Along the wind-scuffed beach, ghosts of the dawn wavering
    over the coldly quiet sea.
"Their little jabbing trick in their moments of
    proud flesh. A woman permits it—
Permits the paddling of hands like a dog's paws
    on her and the jigging dance.
The bone digs for the dog and he pants above it
    like a drunken emperor
Rubbing himself in victory.

                                    "Short, shallow, soon done.
    How they wilt away.
As though they were the satiated conquerors—not
    the possessed and the spat out—
Snore back into dank-breathed sleep. What woman
    could like it and like herself?
Only a wench so hollow she feels empty without it
    to needle her vanity.
Let me be closed and cool and dry.

    "I know his kind, and they are all alike.
Having had it, he'll come sniffing and skulking around
    to snatch an easy piece.
Though Helge might be worse. Was it Helge I wanted
    and took his shadow instead?
But I couldn't have borne his arrogant assurance. He's the
    kind to be ridden Roman and then dismissed.
I'll scare Finboge by looking at Thorvard as though
    Thorvard were a husband—
Which soon for his moment I'd better let Thorvard be.
    I forgot my sterile guard.
Poor clump of a boy, Finboge wouldn't know. Nor know
    that once is always enough for me—
Once now and then with a new one as a reminder
    how weak they are.
But I was a fool to let wine make me forget that
    I need no more reminders.

Let me be left alone. I want to be rinsed head to foot,
  new-clothed and combed and left alone."

"Freydis!"

          "Ah, you startled me, Thorvard."

                                    "Where have
  you been?"

  "How long
Have you roused out of a stupor of sleep, where I saw
  you last, to be asking that?"

"Well, I looked for you."

  "Yes, I daresay. Did you sort that heap of humans
    strewn about?
Look at the pigs! Sodden. Stupid. Wrapped carcasses
    on the ground
As though dragged for our feast but not found fit.
    Did you expect me here?
Whoring, I suppose, like these? Married and unmarried
    in each other's arms,
All gape-mouthed here at the daylight."

  "No, Freydis, but I—"

  "Hush!
It was these and their noise I got away from. I
    rested in somebody's empty house,
Then walked the beach for love of a change of wind.
    It's fresh and clear by the shore,
You ought to try it. Or are you grown pleased with
    this reek? You carry your share."

"Ah, well, it was Yule, Freydis. And everyone was gay.
    Yourself with the rest."

"How dare you throw my name amidst this swine! I'd
    let them freeze

Save there'll be wood to cut and ships to sail. They
    have some use, whipped to it.
Kick them awake. —No, wait. Where are those precious
    brothers, our partners?"

"Oh, many went decently home before dawn, Helge among
    them. Finboge I've not seen."

"Of that one I've a thing or two someday to tell you.
    A pagan prattle
Bubbles up from his liquor. He's maddened with gods-talk."

  "Yet Freydis,
You are not the intensest Christian I've ever known."

  "Be still! Be still!
Can't you open your mouth without offense to me and
    the air I breathe?
And as to the Roman rites, who was it commanded this
    Yule-tide but myself?
None of these excellent converts lying here stiff
    as the ground. No, it was I.
I've myself to thank for this orgy of Christ lovers.
    Behold them—crucified.
I was wise, keeping the camps apart, and a fool gregarious.
Well, we'll have no more of it. You will tell Helge that."

  "Tell him yourself."

For an instant, her face reddening, Freydis regarded
    her husband with tight-lipped fury,
Hating his twitching mouth. And then she said,
    "Very well, then. I shall tell him.
And my own crew will get the same order from me.
    By now they are used to it.
It is not that I am unaccustomed to bearing all the
    work, even when you are sober.

I thought—idly—you might insist upon being your
    own ambassador, Thorvard.
No matter. I'm not Eric's daughter for nothing."

  The risen sun
Rubbed through the morning mists. Pallor of her
    face, the darkness of her eyes
Suddenly illuminated, a gaunt mask mingled of
    venom and fright.
Then the eyes dimmed and drew back a little and the
    face stilled into pride
And that fearsome bravery pride wears as a mask.

  "Only do not bother me now,"
Freydis said, swaying forward a moment as she
    started to walk away.
"Can't you see I am very tired? Get rid of these,"
    she said, gesturing downward.
"Let me be left alone."

V

The cold stretched like a humming drum,
Day after iron day. The woods
Creaked and snapped in the hard air. Bayside
Crusted with great scums of blue-white ice which cowled in
    frozen falls the shore rock.
Sun thin. Night swift in. By night the sky
Vaulting past the northern stars; the stars filmed
With slow clouds of snow.
              Which descended,
Haunting the gray morning, flying, changing
In the wind-music, moaning out of the woods and screaming
    across the waters;
Rolling the world.

  Stormed-in at the fires, the men listening
    to the lash on the roofs

Sat about like large boys without a game; the women
Knelt and prodded at the smoky hearths. Even dark by day,
The huts thickened greasily with cooking stench
    and with people sleeping too much.
Thorvard reported: "There is grumbling among us:
Some say the new-built houses of the Norwegians
    let less to winter than ours.
They say the others are warmer wrapped."

    "Do they propose," asked Freydis, "that we force our
    friends to a swap?"

"One said you could and others seemed to agree."

    "So I had heard. They are restless, aren't they?"

"They tire of snow and darkness and doing nothing."

    "There'll yet be enough to do.
Meat's thin on the hooks. When the weather clears
    we'll have cause for a hurried hunting."

"They grumble at that, too. They say less slaughter
    of trees and more of deer in the fall
Would have been wiser."

    "Then they turn in their talk against me?"

    "No. I dropped a word or two, and now
They say Helge drove his men with such fury we had
    no choice but to match him.
Even now they think he'll outrun us with his greater ship."

    "Good," said Freydis.
"Good that they mistrust him. I like it less,
    though, that they think he calls the tune.
But let them if it sours them."

    The wind thrummed and thudded in the night now
And morning widened to an icy sky.

"This light," Finboge said to Helge on their pathway,
"This light blinds me. As though the sky were
    scoured with light and the earth raised
Radiant."

        "It is very bright," said Helge.

"Like no light elsewhere on earth, Helge.
The whole sky shines and the white land lifts, readied
    for something soon and strange."

"Readier for us, I'd like it. We cannot live on
    snow. If it stays clear—"

                        And it stayed clear,
But with paltry birds in the forest and all fish
    gone out of the sea.
The camps ate poorly, each spoiling with suspicion
    of the other.

On a night knived with sleet, Erling and Thorkel crazily
    plodded toward Freydis' house.

    "I'll be cut in half," Erling gasped.

"Save your breath," said Thorkel.

"I'm doing without as it is. On a fool's errand—what a
    way to die!"

                "Helge knew what he sent, sending us.
Ah, I see firelight."

                "I'm blind—black-blind," said Erling.
    "It's hell you see. Lead me in."

Thorkel said, "Wait—there's a door here somewhere."

    "Do you need a frozen knocker?"
But suddenly—hurled by a blast—the two old sailors
    lurched blinking into the room.

Thorvard cried, "Fasten that door! What do you want here?"

"Who are they?" asked Freydis.

"It's Erling and Thorkel—the other camp."

Freydis came slowly out of remoter shadows,
At first to their wind-slashed eyes a mixture of
    shadows, all scarlet and dusk interwoven.
By the fire, she said, "What do you want here? What do
    you want, intruding like this?
Do you double desertion by a doubling of your own tracks?
    You can stay with the foreigners—hear me?"

And Thorvard: "Speak up! Have you anything to say?"

Winded and weary, Thorkel said,
"Rations, you know, are a scanty event. It goes tough with us.
    We have sleet to drink but little in larder to eat.
The women complain not at all, and some of the men stay
    stout; but many are desperate lean.
Too much desperation begets commoner danger. And we
    thought a community cooking—a sharing
Of such food as there is between the two camps—might
    be an economy of safety for all."

"The speech, I think, is Helge's," said Freydis. "Did
    Helge send you and this supply of words?"

"We thought—Erling and I—as your countrymen—"

"I cannot imagine worse. You have made your choice.
    Have the grace to stay with it.
We lack no less than Helge. But genuine Greenlanders
    differ: we don't beg.
How avid can your masters be? Food, wood, women—never
    enough. They'd forage upon me.
That's their conception of partnership. Thirsty or
    gut-full, they whine with the same wind.

What has your mob been but a heavy hindrance? Tell
    me that," Freydis demanded.
"I led this westward voyage. We have lived here safe
    without Skraelings.
How has Helge helped us? And now he'd have us feed him.
    As for you—traitors and spies—
You Norwegian-loving louts—you sailed with those
    tradesmen, now gnaw with them!"
With cat-like quickness she flung a wire-threaded rope
    and cut their faces with a blow.
"There," she said, "there is some blood to lick. Such as it is."

    Thorvard yanked open the door
And pushed Erling and Thorkel out, latching the leather.
    "I suppose you are right," he said.
"We have fed them in ways enough and with no return. It
    is each for himself."

"Let word of this be known among the men," she said.
    "Ah, we were better alone."

"So the crew feels. They say we'd eat well if there'd
    not been those foreign mouths.
They are restless and quarrelsome."

    "Too much. Too much," said Freydis. "I want no
    trouble now.
Send in the morning a dozen men deeper into the forest."

    And they went,
And others fished the harbor; but bad luck held and
    the food skimped.
Rains kept on, opening the earth again. Axes began
    again. But most of the men
Roved at the hunting, the women with them. The two
    camps like rival packs.

Late in the night Freydis lay sleepless and restless.
The night was a windless silence.
Through the cracks in the hut walls a northern aurora
glimmered, like light along ice,
Powerful enough for Freydis to see shapes and shadows
and beside her open-mouthed Thorvard asleep.

"It may be," she thought, "this waking dream of a death-light,
this waking nightmare of silver horses,
Stallions of light rearing soundless across the heavens,
pawing the underfloors of Valhalla with hooves
Which are only a flutter of pictures—they make no sound—
a dream of wild, sky-tall stallions. But I know,"
She went on thinking, "it's this pulse that's been slipped
inside me and grows in my belly. Will show soon.
I must tell him before he notices, as though it were his.
He'll assume it. Poor Thorvard.
And that Norwegian boy need never know.

"I am sure. I am sure. Yes, I am sure.
And no one need ever know, only myself. It will show
soon. It will move soon.
But already I think I can see it and feel it. Moment
to moment expanding like light in the night.
I burn with it, secretly. Heaviness in me. Evil or good?
Mischance or a fortune? Am I clipped or freed?

"This little Vinlander," she went on thinking. And then she
thought of Gudrid's son Snorre.
A sweat sodden on her neck, she rocked her head, the
black hair a sullen burden.
"Ah!—ah!" she whispered. "This won't be born here,
but he was made here.
He'll be mine—secretly, wholly mine. And he'll be
an Ericson. A sign!" she thought.

"For what will be his through me? Greenland and Vinland.
　　He'll be the only one. The heir to Leif."

Quickly she wakened Thorvard. She told him. And Thorvard
　　held her in his arms though he was at first
Dazed half with sleep—half with her news. "Freydis!
　　Freydis!" he murmured over and over,
All bumbling and proud solicitude after amazement. And
　　in the strange shaking light of the night
He could see that her face bore partly determined glory
　　and partly an ordinary woman's fear.
Never had he felt like this—all concerned and protective
　　man clasping his woman,
His woman defenseless and dear—he there to ward her
　　against the danger he'd done
And with pride in that danger.

　　Though as yet Thorvard was really not thinking; excitement
Was bodily joy, conflagration of blood which began to burn
　　hotter than tenderness,
And Freydis, unlike herself, slowly began threshing against
　　him, and fumbling with hasty, imperative fingers
Bared him and dragged him. His almost immediate spasm
　　seemed to Thorvard
The sign of his fatherhood sealed.

　　Freydis at once slept. Out of her, flung back in
　　labored breathing,
Thorvard was wildly, exultantly awake. His brain like his
　　mouth felt atwitch with the nerves of the world,
His body as though it had taken a flattening blow which
　　gladdened it somehow. And spent,
Spent hollow with feeling of victory, Thorvard smiled to
　　himself, and eyes closed smiled to the night.
"It is joined! It is joined!" he kept thinking.
　　"This child that's to be

Locks me with Leif. The lines are tangled forever. We're
    mingled for good. And this getting
Which I had believed Freydis would never welcome—oh,
    it's done and it's welcomed.
The grandchild of Eric is my child. Where she walks—
    where he walks—all heads will turn round to see.
This is the bond. Now there is no way to lose." But almost
    as if there were, with returning tenderness,
Thorvard held Freydis, now quietly, in his arms. And while
    he was thinking he couldn't yet bear to sleep,
Deeply he slept.

Finboge thin in the starlight with Helge at midnight
    watched the northern aurora
Stalagmitic.
            Uprushing, the columns of pale color
    swayed over the world; the shafted
Unconsuming fire shuddering now in a great arch as though
    shaken with wind-thunder.
Pale red and pale gold and a running of cold-sea blue
    flickering across the gigantic fan
Which filled, faded, and filled. Götterdämmerung.
    Ice-rooted, trumpeting flame,
The living crown of the north fastnesses lifted up
    like a host of fire and held
Wrenching but magneted there between the farthest curve
    of the earth and the sucking sky.
Rivers of gaunt light fed out of hidden caves and
    streaming wildly toward deeper night.
Flecked flame from darkness into darkness flooding—
    trumpets and the rolling undertow of doom,
Like the last colors of life shimmering down to the color of
    death.

    The gray twilight

Rippled on Finboge's face. The brothers stood in an
    open place which was raddled with tree-stumps
Wetted by late-melted snow.

   "If we could leave soon, I should be happy," said Helge.
"At last out of sight of that woman."

   "I've had no sight of her, three months since Yule."

"Be glad of it then, Finboge. —But you are not, are you?
    I warned you against her."

"Cold—cold. She watches in the dark. You are with her,
    but she is not with you."

"I see. I thought as much. Hot women don't leave men
    hungry—and you
Suffer another emptiness than the mouth's."

   "Then why should she want it at all?"

"She wanted it?"

   "Yes. Yule-time."

   "Oh, to watch you in the dark no doubt. Once."

"She is a witch. This whole land is bewitched. I
    thought our ancient gods
Marched at some utter margin which we neared.
    I don't know. —Freydis,
Freydis, Freydis scents this air."

   "Christ forgive you, Finboge."

   "Christ?
That name comes from another land. Here it has a far
    and foreign sound."

               "Never.
Never, if you believe in the true God."

"Let us sail soon," said Finboge. "Can we sail
Whenever we want? Could not Erling and Thorkel—our
    own westward crossing—
Teach us the safe route east again?"

    "Another month, another moon," Helge replied.
"I have talked with them. We must wait out the spring
    storms. And, too,
More wood's to be got to fill the ship. And we should
    be better fed."

"Ah, there's enough cut."

    "We have voyaged too far and sweated too much, Finboge,
Not to take all we can. We talked of kingdoms.
        Well, let us have such booty
As someday we may carry in our hands. And still there's
    Freydis. Good fortune or bad, we are with her.
If she desires both ships to sail together we must
    strive once more to agree.
And there's the look of it, too, in Leif Ericson's eyes."

    "Her worry, I'd think."

"Well, I want not even shadows of trouble with Leif.
    He's a good man."

"I am hollow with hunger."

    "Tomorrow we'll try again. And it's almost tomorrow."

"Morning is over the sea where we came from," Finboge sighed.
    "Ah, soon to return to the sun!"

As they turned toward their houses the night seemed to
    darken behind them.
Now there was only starlight, even in the north. Air cold,
    and the sea brightening strangely.

234

But the sea—the sea
Crawled with long rain through the morning and the day
Poured back into night; the woods
Hummed in the wind, exploded; and another day; and another,
    on the fourth
Through a seeping, twisting drizzle Finboge stumbled
    weakly across headland rock
That between cedar and surf vaulted arches of rust-red granite.
"Withdrawn," he mumbled, glaring at the spindrift curdle.
    "They have gone back.
All the true gods. They were near. We were near.
    They have forsaken us now.
Offense of this Christian smell grew too much. Even
    seaward the air reeks with it.
Sodden with it."

              To the left there was murmur of thunder.
   "The Christian fumblings,
Strong enough to muddle this world but never to hold it.
    Bead-snatchers. Pious insults
To the gods who stand withdrawn—clean and tall in
    the vast arctic shade."

            Shafted,
A shot of sun lanced the horizon edge which closed over.

   Finboge cried out, "O light of Balder!
How dingier your signal blots this air! Oh, name
    this air: Frey's breath. I feel
Loki's fingers locking over my heart!"
                  The sky cracked.
   "Thor! Thor!"
Head back, his upraised arms fisted into the swift
    black air, Finboge screamed.
The massive wall of thunder tumbled forward and the load
    of rain was loosed with a crash. Gashed

With wind-shaken flashes.

    Toward evening—cleared to a lemon light low on the sea—
Coming through wet-whispering brush and out of the
      fragrance-dripping cedars,
Helge, with Erling and Thorkel, found him there stretched
      on the headland rock and soaked
As rubbish thrown from the waves. He did not answer
      his name. When they lifted him up
His eyes seemed not to know them. And his harsh
      breathing muttered a guttural madness.
Suddenly: "I have been praying, Helge. It is a tiring
      trade. I am very tired."

"Come, we will take you home," said Helge. And to his
      companions: "Do not be frightened.
His belly feeds on his brain. Help me, Erling."

    And as they led him, Thorkel behind them
Saw offshore a rounded mass rolling far out in the tide;
      not rock nor ship, something
Slowly wheeled by the waves which the night shut out.
      He resolved on morning. And early
In the chill bright day, yelling and running, Thorkel
      waked both camps with his cries—
"A whale! A whale cast up by the sea! A whale!"

    Out of all the houses,
Pale with sleep but wide-eyed with famine, half-dreaming,
      in dazed elation,
Scrambled the men and women. "Take kettles and water!"
      called Freydis. "Here, Thorvard":
Seizing a long brand from the night's fire, she handed
      him another, and all
Hurried down to the red rocks and the beach beyond.
      At the tide-rim, the mountainous carcass.
With knives, with axes even, the men attacked the

dead monster—cut and coiled the enormous food.
Almost a silent orgy of eating but for the fires' humming
    and the cauldron-seethe.
Hours of it as the morning sun silvered the sky flawless
    and blazed hot on the stony shore.
Gorged at last, they sat or sprawled—eying the scarred
    whale with a bilious content:
Further feasts to come.

  "For the sea's benevolence," said Thorvard, "let us
      thank God."

"Thank Thor!" Shrill as a new whip Finboge's voice
    leaped across them;
Even before their eyes turned to where Thorvard stood
    they swerved to Finboge, risen.
"This reward was cast ashore for the prayer I made
    to my patron god.
Thor has never forsaken us. He is quick with aid.
    He is no laggard Christ!"

                    "Finboge!"
His brother's cry roared over the tumult and a woman's
    "Let us do as he says:
Praise Thor for the food given!"

  "Silence!" It was Freydis' command and in a
      murmuring moment secured.
In the intense stillness of noon Finboge, with the reckless
    joy of a child sure of his virtuous act,
Gazed over the crowd to the tall dark woman. She ran
    a hand through her haggard hair
And stared at the young man awaiting her smile.

  "My brother is ill,"
Helge said. "He means no harm."

  "No harm, indeed! Blasphemy is harmless then?"

At Freydis' words Finboge's face fixed an astonished anger.
   Yet it was that blind moment
He saw the beginning arch of her belly—and knew with his
   flesh the seed of it; knew,
So sure, he shook between sickness and desire; felt that
   all eyes had seen them and known.

   Except perhaps Helge, who said,
"He but lapses into an old naming for the hands and
   feet of the Christ."

"I heard what he said," shouted Freydis. "How does anyone
   dare in the name of the false gods
To profane my new land? Are you not King Olaf's tribe?"

   "We are staunch Christians, Freydis.
You know that," Helge said. "Baptised in the faith
   well before Greenlanders."

"Then maybe newer converts are easier tricked. Your
   brother has a strange way of praying."

"And you a strange way of not," Finboge cried.

   "Insult a woman if you will, but let me say
I should deal death with my own hand to hear a
   pagan yell mouthed of this air.
Do you forget Leif Ericson? He has not grown so meek
   as to suffer sacrilege.
This land is signed with the Cross that stands on
   Thorvold's grave. Men speak of it.
He died in Christ. I would rather retreat to Greenland,
   boats empty—voyage profitless—
Than have this air stained by such desecrant lips!"

   Over the stilled crowd
Freydis and Finboge glared at one another. Disturbed
   at the side of each,
Thorvard and Helge.

238

"Talk on: you have eaten well," Finboge said,
And with a boy's bravado wheeled and strode away inland.

"Freydis—"

"And what more have you to say, Helge?"

"Let us take what remains and cast it into the sea."

Freydis said nothing.

"Come," said Helge. Cowed, wretched, frightened,
    the men and women of his crew
Rose heavily and followed him out on the wet waste
    of the low-tide beach.
Soon others followed—all—Thorvard too—only Freydis
    left—hurled the whale meat away.
Expressionless, Freydis regarded them. Returning, several
    writhed with sickness and vomited
The food they had eaten. Many knelt to ask forgiveness
    of Christ—a few eagerly.

Startled at the hard sound and bewildered, all looked up
    to the rock where Freydis stood
And heard—certain of it now—her wild laughter. Still
    silent they watched her go,
A glimmer of dark red cloak through the cedars and the
    shrill laughter thrown back.

And soon the night came on, glittering over the high,
    deserted beach, the coast rock,
Stringing, interlacing the deep mesh of its stars; the
    continent line ridged with foam:
Vinland-America a sleeping, viviparous mass rolled up
    from the ocean bed, something
The sea begot of the torturing of its depths and lunged
    mammoth against the night—
Long-lolling at the wave-reach and, forested, looming
    athwart the western, unknown sky;

And now sparked—niched infinitesimally—by two small
      stars of campfire at the water's edge.
Strangers there in restless sleep.

V I

And all these things the skald sang in the
      halls of Greenland
Long after these things but long ago; and told how
After the day of the whale the rivers and ocean gleamed
      thick with fish,
Birds came and their eggs whitened the islands, game
      rustled fatly in trees,
And the strangers ate well. The work in the woods resumed
      the separate race for plunder.
But not many days. The days were running out.

   And in these days more than ever Thorvard
Grew an imp of industry, everywhere nimble with orders; and
      Freydis being seldom seen, he was ubiquitous bantam,
At once managerial and imperial: all his small ways
      waxed eager and confident.
He was a wasp in the sun, which filled now with the shimmer
      of birds and new leaves and the fragrance of earth.
The world through which Thorvard went trotting shone silver
      and pink, gold and gold-green; and the sea
Flashed its uncountable diamonds; air all a shot-silk
      of salt and a rumor of rose-leaves,
And the mornings a mingling of gull-wings and song of the
      meadow-larks. Cold smell of felled wood.

The loading of timber began, while cutting continued. And one
      morning as Helge and some of his crew worked by the shore,
A sudden raw sound as of wind across great reeds
Rattled like whips upon stone. Low in the water, not
      far out, a dozen boats rode up the bay,

Black-pelted men in them, Skraelings, each man swift
    at an oar, and tall poles
Swung aloft from the boats' sides: it was these made the
    menacing whirr in the air.
Thigh-deep in the tide the Norwegians stood terror-stunned,
    as though they were strangers discovered at
    thieving in daylight;
Paralysis froze them, mouths gaping and eyes unbelieving
    the boats lifting steadily onward.

                   Then Helge,
As all backed warily toward the beach, said to a stout
    man named Thorbrand,
"Hurry to the hut and sound the horn. The men will come
    from the forest. Send the women inside."
The rest stayed near a few axes and spears on the sand.
    The boats nearer in. Thorkel whispered,
"They make no cries at all and I think their sunward poles
    are a sign of peace."

              "The white shield," said Helge.

Finboge ran downshore to a moored longboat, and as he
    returned with the shield, Skraelings
Were leaping into the outer waves—their boats left
    swaying—and they slogged ahead, weaponless.
As they came—forty or fifty—dripping with sea, Helge swung
    up the white shield, old Viking signal of friendship,
And this too was seen by the gathering Greenlanders
    and Norwegians behind them, though some carried
    spears and swords.
The Skraelings, at first silent, stared brazenly curious
    but with no enmity
Though they were fierce-eyed. They were dark-skinned, stark-
    naked, hairy and thickset, broad-faced and strong.

"Here," Helge said: "Here," and gave them the white shield
    which shone like an Amazon breast.
Then the savages broke into babbles of wonder, and handed
    the shield about, fondling the leather and metal.
Several ran, as if at command, back into the waves and
    pulled boats ashore: small, with skin hulls.
Amidst paddles, poles, some fashion of slingshots, there
    were furs in two of the boats, and a Skraeling
    grasped a great gray fell
And, grinning, dropped it at Helge's feet.

  By now the women had timidly come to the beach; and,
    tardily, Thorvard
Without Freydis, who was not to be seen, pushed through the
    throng and halted by Helge's side. The Skraelings
Having made their gift proceeded to bargaining. From the boats
    they brought other furs, gesturing happily toward them,
Then gesturing toward the Norse weapons.

  "None of that," said Helge, shaking his head.

  Thorvard said, "I agree."

One of the blackest of Skraelings, who gleamed as though
    greased, seemed alarmingly nakeder when he darted
Into the Greenlanders' group and clutched the red skirt
    of one of the women.

                    "Stop him!" Thorvard shouted.

"Wait!" said Finboge. "It isn't the woman he wants—
    he's asking for cloth. See his face."

So some of the women went and fetched bolts of the red weave
    they had woven and dyed through the winter days
And Norwegians and Greenlanders traded cuts of the cloth for
    a bale of furs; even when the cloth ran short
Skraelings with innocent joy swapped for the hand-sized
    swatches; though again

One or another would touch a sword or a spear like persistent
   children with an evident glance of guile.
The talk among them seemed to be of the weapons and some of
   them looked sullen, but all at once
Bearing their shares of the red foreign weaving and the
   white shield of peace,
They drew their boats out beyond waves, clambered in
   and silently rowed south out of sight.

"Well," said Finboge with an impertinent look to Thorvard,
   "so we are safe here from Skraelings?"

But Helge broke in: "This is no time for ragging. We've
   troubles enough to decide. Where is Freydis?"

"Freydis is unwell," said Thorvard; "I will speak for her."

   And not to alarm the crews
Who after excitement began to be alarmed, Helge and Thorvard
   and Finboge went aside; Helge talking:
"This is a worrisome business. That went well enough. But
   the danger's apparent. Those filthy black savages—
Who's to say when they'll return? Our question is: Shouldn't
   we board the two ships and sail at once?"

Thorvard gazed up the beach to the great ships anchored close
   in now: hawk-beak and dragon-head reared in the noon.
"Neither is more than half-loaded," said Thorvard.

   "Better a half going safe home," Helge said, "than
   dead here with none."

"We outnumber them," Thorvard said.

   "I think we should go," said Finboge.

   "And we have the weapons," Thorvard went on.
"These seemed without bows and arrows even."

"This day—this day," said Helge. "But what do we
know of them? Their weapons? Their numbers?"

"I know how Freydis will feel," said Thorvard. "We are so
nearly ready. She could not bear it
To cut to a half all that we've worked so hard for. Think—
only a few days more—we can post a guard, day and night—
Speed the work on and be gone soon. And as for the Skraelings—
they are bargain-delighted enough for the time being."

But Thorvard was wrong. Next morning, before the Norwegian
stationed on a headland could wind his horn,
The Skraelings themselves gave warning: a screaming chant as
their rapid boats came on, more boats than before:
Their poles slanted down—turned from the sun—and the
venomous scream ululating over the ocean like victory.
As all the Norse rushed together to the beach an old sailor
raised a red shield, bloody, gigantic eye.
Still offshore the Skraelings hurled from skins on the
poles a rain of stones.
These clouted like hard hail among the whites who could
not retaliate. Massed crews and their leaders
Backed perhaps twenty paces and stood by a massive rock—
easy targets, with spears poised.
The women had hidden in the woods. Reconnoitering slowly,
the men, still backing, followed.

As the Skraelings, slinging more stones and screaming the
wilder, rushed in a tumult to shore
The Norse spears sang into them. Several fell, but they
seemed a swarm, everywhere,
Too far for sword-reach and too close for arrows, and the
shingle itself to arm them.
Outnumbered and stunned and confused, Norwegians and
Greenlanders broke, ran toward the forest.

244

Freydis yelled—no one heard her—"Cowards!
   Sick though I am,
Had I a sword I would fight in the place of ten of you!"

   She was entering the woodside,
Following the other women; moved slowly and painfully.
   Men stumbled around her.
But the Skraelings were gathering stones on the shore.
   Freydis pitched—crawled past the farthest stumps.
And someone—a woman from the other camp—dragged her in
   by the hand. She stood hard-winded against a tree,
Her eyes in a blaze of fury fit to consume countrymen,
   Norwegians, and foe—all or any alive.

There were arrows and bows in the woods—carried in
   by the women.
But now there came pause in the battle. Reassembled,
   the routed surveyed the enemy.
The Skraelings were kicking aside fallen spears—could not
   use them—and several
Passed an ax back and forth—tried it against driftwood—
   and seemed to marvel
At the cutting slug of the blade. One smashed the skull
   of the dead Greenlander
Whose ax it had been. Then another seized it and
   struck it against a boulder;
The iron broke on the stone. Several chattered in new
   amazement, and then they laughed.
They tossed the iron pieces into the water. Then all
   gathered as if for a charge uphill.

The stout man, Thorbrand, lay dead almost at the woodside—
   a stone stuck in his eye,
His sword flung beside him. As the Skraelings rushed,
   Freydis moved out like a tranced woman,
Gray in the face—hair mad—the bodice torn full off
   her great breasts.

She seized the huge sword. Turning she screamed
    at the Skraelings,
And wildly advancing, she struck the blade flat to her
    naked flesh. They stopped—slings slack,
And in that moment an arch of arrows curved from the woods
    and shattered upon them.
Crying out, they turned heel, fled to their boats and
    were soon gone.
A dozen—all but two of them Skraelings—were dead at
    the tide-rim, Thorbrand on the hillside.
And Freydis spun to the grass and lay like the dead. It was
    Finboge helped Thorvard carry her to the house.

And now dissension and panic afire in the two camps
    ran like a crazing assault.
They were victors together of temporary victory; nearly worse
    —they knew—than defeat. For revenge any moment
Could strike in more terrible numbers, and they had seen
    the ax break on the stone.
Because the three dead were Norwegians all, their fellows
    now bitterly claimed they were used as a shield
Cleverly by the Greenlanders; Greenlanders growled that
    Helge had handled all rudely:
Had a weapon or two been traded, then where was the harm,
    and the Skraelings would not have returned,
Or not as their enemies. Even some scufflings between them
    had to be pacified—even among women—
For there were those unexpectedly cool—Thorkel and Erling
    for two—who knew that the danger was shared;
Danger they had in common.
                   And then there was much to do,
    bruised and afraid though they were:
Helge let it be known they would sail on the following
    morning at the turn of the tide;
They had only to pray the Skraelings off—he said—till
    that early hour, and the chances seemed fair.

This was agreed—he said—with Thorvard, remaining by
    Freydis' bedside, she still in her deep swoon.
Dead Skraelings could lie where they were, like the carrion
    they were, but Norwegians decently buried.
So this was done. And all the day long the crews—and the
    women with them—came and went at the ships,
Loading possessions, more timber, all they could, till sundown.

    Still Freydis lay like the dead,
And there was death in her—the child; and when death
    flooded it from her it awoke her.
Though for a time she stayed with eyes so widely black
    they seemed not to see,
While Thorvard, assisted by a woman of their camp, attended
    upon her—Thorvard in sickened despair,
The forged chain of his eminence fragments before him.
    And for a time when the woman departed
There was great silence everywhere—guards posted, but camps
    in exhausted slumber—and silence trembling in the room.

"Is it gone? Has it left me? I'm empty now?"—Freydis had
    turned her head toward Thorvard, her eyes
Unchanging; they seemed not to see. Light from the fire in
    the room—it was the one fire that night in Vinland—
Fluttered across them as across basalt eyes, lidless and
    ancient, of a queen long perished.

"My son," said Thorvard. "My son that had never lived is dead."
    And more than their habit, his lips shook. He regarded
As if for denial or comfort the white mask, black-haired
    on the bed.

"He was nothing of yours. He was all mine," said the face,
    and became Freydis. She stared at him.
"Now I must go to the ship," she said, not moving.

    "It is scarcely the middle of night," said Thorvard;
"We've hours of waiting and you had better sleep." And that
    was the last he said for a long while,

247

For Freydis muttered on and on like one in a dream: voice
  never raised, body unmoving:

"It is time that I went to the ship if I'm to die with him.
  Who else could it be? What other maiden than I?
Who served him but I? Would you lift me? No—no. Let me
  down. Nobody carries Freydis. I can walk there.
Did you think I unwillingly go? I am his sister and nearest.
  I know where my place is. My Lord Leif.
His body expects me. Have you decked him out? He must wear
  most radiant robes. He was a king. But of course you know.
On the ship he is stretched now under the tent high
  on that wood. Fire to come, but myself first.
He dreamed Christ had him, but death gives him to me, and
  we'll burn in the heart of death in the old way.
Such prominent death— What was that fighting? No matter.
  Such prominent death floods all their air,
Breathes into all nostrils. That pyre will burn up this land;
  and those of you left to watch shall have smoke for
  your breathing.
We'll make a cairn of this land, of wood and ashes; and
  only the stones will remember.

"Death in the dark. I could not see it but it was hurtful.
  How can a woman long for rape and be raped?
Yet it was that at last. The brute hooking, myself at last
  powerless. O sweet surrender of dying!
Now the pain is gone and I feel so hollowed out.

"Where? —Yes. To the ship, I said.
Have you placed his sword at his side? And his other
  ancestral weapons, the axes, the spears?
His face will be blackening now—I have seen many a corpse—
  and we'll have a kindred look, Leif and I;
All but that toss of silver and gold hair. I have a manacled
  feeling—I shine bright with chains!

248

O everything shines so, now it is morning. What glitter of
   sun on the sea! What a day to voyage!

"Who are the tall naked boys riding the two black stallions
   up the surf-edge? Do I know them? No matter.
They ride hard with the wind at their yellow hair. When the
   horses falter, kill them for honor of Leif. It is custom.
Send the boys to me when their elders come.

                              "Wine! This
   bowl is not to be drained while I still live.
My head whirls with it. Pour the bloody—sweet, sweet
   bloody veins of this country whose name I forget.
The girl who dies with her lord dies drunk forever. I
   suck at an endless vine twisted in rock.
Have you taken him food? The breads and the venison?
   Food has been plentiful lately with us. Mingle it
There with his helpless weapons. The slaughtered hen, the
   cleft cock, the sundered dog—all at his feet.
Soon—I. Soon—I. Will you kill the great horses now?
   Now you may lift me up with your dirtied hands
For I breathe the ecstatic and fishy smell of death like
   a white spume through the air.

"Listen! I see Eric my father but no woman beside him.
   He is my one begetter. Lift me again.
I should see my kinsmen—there's nothing but sand and a
   swirling of ocean and rain. Again.
Ah! I see Leif Ericson living. He waits there impatiently.
   Now I must go to the ship.
Summon a strong hag to be angel of death—to be quick
   when the time comes.

"I am the angel of—no; no. Is this wine cold enough?
   I'm muddled with heat of it. More!

"Bare me with gentleness now that I lie here. It's likely
   the last I'll know and the first I recall.

You are the first to perform the rest of the business, aren't
    you? One moment. And you'll not be gentle at that.
Are there many will take me? The leaders, the potent elders.
    I suppose Helge and Finboge; Thorvard perhaps
And a dozen besides. For the love of me and to send me to
    Leif streaming with life. Each of you—once.
Wait for a moment. Remember I do this in the name of
    the dead. Your hands
Are so massive and heavy. Ah! The bearded and long weight.
    What stranger are you? No—no; —no matter;
    meat's nameless.
Ah, now! I am filled with—impaled with—ah! ah!
    Now—now—now!"

                    Until now unmoving,
Freydis in thrash on the bed seemed to the terrified Thorvard
    crouching beside it maybe to wake
Out of her dream of death, for her eyes closed, and she seemed
    to him racked toward the conscious and real night.
And when her moans ended, her eyes shifted with a seeking
    look—not fixed as they were before.

"I am the angel of death. Tie the slut tight. Stand away.
    Was it twelve—was it twenty—had her?
Here's a wiltless dagger will match her a plunging for each.
    It is iron will tickle her now.
Take that, my girl! Take that from an old woman's fist!
    Ah, you don't cry out for this fellow.
He's a boy sleepless and twenty, can do and do what he's done.
    And bequeath you to Leif."

Again indrawn like a rattle of nightmare, Freydis' breath
    made a shuddering silence of shadows. She said:
"If I am nearest of kin it's my duty to fire this death-ship.
    But if I am Freydis then how am I

This naked youth blessed with the sway-sag at the groin,
   the torch thundering high in the beach-wind?
While the crews watch me, awaiting this fiery ending.
   No. No! The wood must not burn! The wood is mine!
No! I am Freydis—Freydis—Freydis!"

   Thorvard grasped her as she writhed upward and turned
      as to leave the bed.
"Hush!" he said. "Hush! You have been dreaming."

   Staring at him, she asked, "Have I been drinking much wine?
I feel as though I have been very drunken. I ache so
   and am so sodden in sweat."

He repeated: "You dreamed wildly and talked.
   Don't you remember?"

   "No," she said, "I don't seem to. I—
Oh, yes. I remember it now. I was sick. I fought off the
   Skraelings. My child was murdered somehow.
Is the cargo safe? Is this still the night of the day
   we're to sail for Greenland?"

"Yes. Yes. You must rest, Freydis. You are all right again."

   Instantly her eyes flickered a cold cunning.
"Finboge fathered it," she said, smiling.

                           "What do you mean?"

   "Finboge did your work for you once."

"You liar! You liar! He was mine! You would not have let—
   Freydis, you're mad, saying that!"

"No—I'm all right again, just as you've said."

                           "It was force?"

   "How else? You know me. And how could I tell you?
But now it's no matter—unless you'd like to kill Finboge?"

"Oh, God! Oh, God! I won't believe this!"

"Although," she went on, "the killing of Finboge now might
start more blood than it stopped. It's hardly convenient."

Thorvard, quieter all at once, said, "What have I left?"
his voice that of a man scuttled of bone.

"Well, you have me," she said. "Or, there's divorce.
Really, I shouldn't like it. And Leif wouldn't.
Oh—I dreamed Leif was dead: did I tell you? I can't
recollect the rest of it. I suppose
I became ruler of Greenland. A sign, do you think?"

"If he forced you, I'm sickened enough.
That arrogant, oily adolescent. He's hardly twenty. A
sallow Norwegian dog I should split.
That it was his blood—blood such as that—not mine—
oh, no—I will not believe it. I feel dirtied
Believing such mockery."

"Shall I bring him to you?"

"Bring him here?"

"Here and unarmed. You could scarcely go there with a sword."

"He'd be missed when we sail."

"Leave this to me. He came stumbling here, sick. And with
Christian forbearance we carried him to our ship
Where I am a model of nursing and he's too sick to be seen.
Helge soon hears he has died. And he's wrapped
All but the face for sea burial. Have a care where your
blade cuts."

Thorvard looked dazed. But he said:
"Too simple."

"Your only danger is Helge for moments this morning.
And Helge, I tell you, has plenty to busy him."

252

"Yes—that is true. But—but you have no strength for
  such errands."

                    "You said yourself I'm all right again.
I have strength for an errand that's waited a long time.
  You wait here and see."

All the days were run out. And the nights had gathered
  at last into the last.
The night tall with moonlight—late light long past
  midnight; false dawn
Casting a rippling shadow of wind in the eastern woods,
  but the sky brightness
All the insulation of moonlight still, and the two
  clusters of houses held. No sound,
Only the sea moving a little in sleep. The death-light
  a wide, effortless snare:
A ghost as of memory of snow on the land and glitters
  of ice burning under the sea.

  Freydis
Appeared from her house alone. Only two Greenlanders,
  guarding the headland, saw her.
Crossing the misted slope of the stump-studded meadow
She strode like her own shadow, like a woman shaped of night,
Hurrying with bare feet through the new grass, her robe
  blowing against her;
She came to the dark house of the two brothers Helge and Finboge
And stood quietly at the half-opened door.

Then she pushed the door wider; at first seeing nothing, she
Felt the inward dusk alive with the breathing of many
  sleepers. But a man near the door
Rose clumsily; whispered, "Freydis? What do you want here?"
  And coming toward her was Helge.

After a moment she said, "I want to talk with you. Come out
with me." And she led the way
A few steps to a log east of the house.

"You are ill?"

"I have been. But I'm all right again."

"You can't be," he said. "Even in this light I can see
you've a haggard look."

"How I look is no matter; and no concern of yours that I've
ever heard, Helge. Where's Finboge?"

"Sleeping, poor fellow. Half-dead like the rest."

"Half-dead?" She smiled. "I, too. I, too."

Staring at her warily, curiously, Helge said, "I have had no
sleep. You choose an odd hour to talk."

"It is urgent," she said.

"You know that Thorvard and I have settled to sail
with the morning tide?"

"So he says. I consented. We must, I suppose." Freydis
stood up, clutching her robe in the moonlight.
"Helge," she said, "will you change ships with me? You've
the larger ship—I've the larger crew."

Still asquat on the log, peering at Freydis as at a riddle,
Helge said, "What sort of business is that?
I've more than enough men to sail my ship to Greenland. If we'd
half the men—and thank God, despite the Skraelings,
We're not reduced to that—both ships could still sail.
Ah," he said, "I know you well by now, Freydis.
You've an itch for a larger cargo—which I doubt that I carry.
But you—you'd never believe me.

254

No. You must be queen even of a wilderness—even of a stack
  of lumber. What useless zeal!
We've had our troubles and quarrels in Vinland, and most of
  them spurred by your greed and distrust.
Now that it's over, Freydis, I'll tell you that. Now at least
  we're to get away, and the most of us living.
And at least, uninfected, there's the bargain to share what we
  took. From Leif down, everyone's witness,
And that you can't alter."

  Freydis shook as if in terror or anger. "Helge," she said,
  "I will pay.
Sail as you like but let me have the two cargoes. I must have
  all. Do you understand? I will pay."

Helge stood up, but half turning as though to return to his
  house. He said, "Freydis, I am a man of business.
That means I'm a man of my word—given and taken. In all
  fairness—however the wood is carried—
I'll make equal division with you at the Greenland shore. And
  there's a decent end to this wretched wrangling.
It's better than you deserve but not than I. Nor, I guess,
  than Thorvard. I doubt if you'll see it so.
And now I must rest."

  "As you say, then," Freydis replied. "As you say."
  She stared off
At the whitened rim of the moon, hill-gnawed and
  pitching down. Her voice
Sounded as though the irresponsible dead spoke between
  night and morning. But saying no more, she turned
In the quickened air beginning to trouble the east and
  she strode away to her house,
Entered the dim room, shut the door, stood a rigid moment
  gazing at Thorvard who sat

Head in hands near the fire, his sword on the earth beside
   him. As he grasped it, he looked slowly.
"Freydis!" he said. "What is it, Freydis? You are alone?
   What has happened?"

"I'll be avenged for this," she said. "And I'll be avenged
   now, in this place. Do you hear me?
Ah, I feel how far I have come from home, where men still
   honor the daughter of Eric.
Thorvard, I swear I will leave you—all Greenland shall
   blush with this shame and with yours—
If this unbearable last abuse goes unavenged. I have borne
   too much. I went to those brothers
And offered in peace to pay for their ship—"

   "To buy their ship?"

   "That you and I
Might reap the fortune deserved."

                              "Finboge—?"

   "I tell you, it was Helge insulted me and abused me.
Finboge, Helge, where's the difference when deviltry's in
   the wind? Finboge's only the dog at Helge's heels.
   Don't you want the master?
They threaten us. We are not safe even for sailing. But I'm
   too shrewd for the lot. I know what they plan.
Come with me, Thorvard. Stay with me now if you want
   to stay any longer. Come!"

Wrenching away, she ran out of the house, Thorvard following
   ungainly with his sword and as if in a dream.
"Quickly!" she said; and her face was tearless and cold. And
   together, from house to house, they wakened their crew,
Most of them gaping at Freydis as though she had risen from the
   dead; she whispering over and over,

"Quickly! Take arms and come. The Norwegians are plotting
     against us. It is our death or theirs.
Do you hear me? Bring axes and swords. These foreigners hope
     for Skraelings—to join them. Quickly!
They plot to delay us—to set the savages on us. Hurry if you
     love your lives! We must strike first! Do you hear me?"

They hurried stumbling with swords and axes into the
     brightening day,
And to the silent houses of the Norwegians. All in a
     few dazed minutes.
"Seize them," said Freydis. "Bind them with your belts.
     Lead them out one by one."

The men rushed into the houses while Thorvard stood
     uncertainly at his wife's side.
Clatter, outcries and the thud of fists, but little of that,
     so swiftly were the Norwegians seized asleep
And were pushed groping and dumb forth to
     a nightmare of morning.

Most fell like struck oxen. Those writhing out of hand
     were soon hacked down.
Repeated crunch of iron into skull stilled their yells,
     the last groaning sounds
Were cut. Helge and Finboge and all the others:
     slowly unfurling
A wide red cloak of blood on the Vinland ground.

     Yet whimpering moans and cries
Sounded in one of the houses. A sailor said, "The five
     women are in there.
We have bound them. Where shall we take them?"

     Studying what sprawled strewn upon the grass
As though intent upon making a certain count, Freydis at
     first seemed not to hear.

Then she turned to the man and with a small smile—her
    hand extended—commanded,
"Give me your ax." And Freydis went into the house.
    The men bespelled,
Their weapons wet at their sides, heard the shrieks and
    the drumming death
Now for the first time.

    The trembling of her hands and the blood on her
      bare feet betrayed her
Only a little. As she walked past the men she looked
    no more at the slain.
And when Thorvard and the rest followed her silently back
    through the field
At her own doorway she faced them and their women
    huddled nearby.
Her eyes seemed sightless yet roved sharply among them.

    "These bloody deaths," she said,
"Forced ax and sword upon our hands. We did not willingly
    reach for them.
Remember that. I see horror clawing the eyes of some; fear
Flogging some throats here. But look, breathe, and be glad.
It might have been otherwise. This rising sun was sure
    of blood to dry.
Well, it's not yours—not yours. Remember that.

    "We have all that they meant to filch.
Pretended friends and partners—ah, they always coveted all.
This ground has eaten better men, but let them feed it.
Us it will richly feed, and our right was the real right
    from the beginning.
We can sail now with a treasure that's all for Greenland.
    At once, we must board both ships."

    Her face stiffened.

258

"We are all together in this. Remember that. The deaths
    of the foreign women,
Those, too, had to be. This you will understand but none
    of it might be understood at home.
Treachery, deceit and a mad plan of avarice: how should
    these be bodied and believed?
We'll credit Skraelings' justice—or a disease that
    favored Norwegians only—or a whale eaten
Only by Norwegians, greedy, unpraying. For who, not one
    of us, would realize our justice?
—Yes, that will do."

    Suddenly upflinging her hands, her voice a great cry:
"I'll have the heart of any who tells of this. See that we
    stay together. The rewards are for life, for all.
Let no man speak in Greenland of these things."

VII

"Fire," Leif Ericson said, "has pared the bone white
    from the stinking flesh.
So the rotted stench of the past months, murmurous
    with rumor, gives up its gas;
Breath of murder, and named—the name Freydis."

    Alone, he stalked the room by the one window
From which he could stare at the new cairn on the hillside:
    stone heaped, the grave of his old dwarf Tyrker
Overlooking the ocean from Brattahlid. The year late.
    The day late. The air
Brittle and bright with multitudinous arrows of light,
    hurtling out of the west.
The vacant and wide waters a hammered gold.

    "Fire," Leif Ericson said,
"Singeing the foot, licking at armpit and groin, bored
    into the eye: that hell

Flushes the secrets of the heart and brain. So I have
    them now for my own.
Brute—brute. May Christ forgive me! How shall I
    sleep again? How can she sleep?
Scorn, venom and horror attend her like filthy hags;
    scream in the night. Their arrogance
Outdoes her, even. My own sleep long since a torture
    with what I guessed: will knowledge
Banish or increase that secret fire?

    "Monk-heart-searcher Christ hold the hawk-seat.
But circling above this treachery and ruin? Can that
    wing-beat cool this burning?
Violence is begotten out of violence and where's it to
    finish unless Christ forgive me?
My house is a black scar on the falling sun, as if it
    were flame-eaten.
My hands are black with the brands I held against naked
    men to make them babble.
Now I know all they knew. How shall I sleep? What shall
    I say to her?
Is this sea deep enough to cleanse my hands? It floods
    with that dark and poisonous blood
Washing with every tide over the long path from Vinland,
    and scums our doorsills.

"Her sill untrodden now. How could I not have known?
    The two of them—Thorvard with her—
Stripping their rooms in hysterias of giving to those
    who came back. The Vinland timber
Stacked unsold in her fields. Her gaiety—then her silence—
    then her hiding. The lies
Of select disease, of the Skraelings—then silence. Silence:
    the purr of bribery stroking truth.
Which now I have put the torch to and fouled my own hands.

"Out of my houses,
All this out of my houses. What did I give her, giving
her roofs and walls?
All that was always mine was partly hers. What more did
the woman want?
Finboge prattling of active and thoughtless gods found
favor with her. But so did Helge seem wise,
Talking of kingdoms of the ax and the Cross. And did I, too,
talking of swords and the Cross?
And now no ax, no sword, no gods, no Cross—she is
emptied, alone,
Because she coveted all.

"Half-child, half-sister; she brought forth death.
Now—now—
No; I cannot do what I might. Exile at home will do
and do enough.
If Christ forgive her then must I forgive her? If I
forgive her then does He shrive me?
Where does forgiveness begin?"

As Leif stood at the window hearing the words of his
thought, he did not hear
A servant's steps on the stone floor behind him; but turned
vacantly when the man touched his sleeve.
"Sir, there is ugly news. Thorvard of Gardar is dead. His
throat cut and the knife in his own hand."

"Thorvard? Thorvard?" said Leif. And then in a moment:
"Perhaps it is better so; even though that way.
I'd not have thought him cruel by himself—or to himself.
Or was it a careful kindness?
God rest the man. I never understood him but I think he
intended no harm. Where's Freydis?"

The door, like an answer to Leif's question, clanged in the
corridor; then there came

The slow scuff, as of an aged walking by rote—an uncertain
   and groping scuff, and Freydis
Came wandering into the room wearing a bright red robe
   and it made the stranger
Her wild dark eyes for seeming the only part of her
   that was still alive. Involuntarily
Leif for a second turned again to the window but then, as
   the servant departed, faced Freydis.

In a kind of recognition there was a small grin, as she
   said, "I have come to show you my new dress.
Do you like it? Your mother made it herself. There was
   nobody'd do it for me. I can't
Seem to find anyone will do a thing for me now. Do you
   like it? I picked the color myself."
And she held the skirt wide and moved slowly around for
   him to see it. Head cocked
In a travesty-flirtation, she peered up at Leif and smiled
   at him again. "I think it becomes me.
Red's for black hair, you know. Now you—you inherited
   gold, and that's a different story.
I'll make you a cloak someday—a great blue cloak to fit
   those shoulders and suit that Norwegian hair.
But I have so much to do. It seems as though everything's
   left to me. And I'm very tired."

While Leif listened, his face a contorted bewilderment,
   comprehension and slow dismay,
Freydis was never still: hands heavily ringed, braceleted
   arms of astounding pallor, fluttering,
And as though all had faded to whiteness save the wild dark
   eyes and the dead black hair.
He decided to speak sharply: "Sit down, Freydis." And in
   unaffected surprise she obeyed.

"Freydis," said Leif, "do you know about Thorvard?"

"Thorvard."

"Your husband, Freydis. Were you there?
Where have you been? After all, whatever he meant to you,
Thorvard is dead."

She stared with inquiring calm. She said, "Of course. Oh,
I seldom think of him now, but now and then
Of course I remember. How strange of you, asking me that.
For he wasn't your father. I've told you";
Suddenly shaken by a silent laughter, said, "In my old age
I'm a truthful gabber. Although,
I guess I'm not very old."

"Freydis," he said. "What do you remember? Do you
know me? I am Leif."

"Yes. You are Leif.

"You remember Vinland?"

From squinting toward the bright window, she shifted
her glance,
Now half-blinded, toward Leif again. "That was a bad omen,"
she said. "When your grandfather's horse stumbled.
Leif's ship was readied to sail for Vinland—the first time.
Didn't I ever tell you about it?
He'd got the ship from a Norwegian trader named Biarne
Heriulfson—a great fool of a man.
Biarne was first to set sight on the shores of Vinland.
But, off his course, he was sailing for Greenland.
When he saw through the tearing fog firred hills and wide
fields, Biarne was wise with suspicion it wasn't Greenland."
Freydis shook again with inaudible mirth. "So Biarne
kept sailing and got here.
He told solemnly all misadventures, and that," she said,
"is how Leif heard of the western lands.

From a stupid Norwegian.—But what was I going to tell
you? Oh, yes. The bad omen.
So Eric—my father—rode his horse toward Ericsfiord,
planning to voyage with Leif;
But his horse stumbled—a sign from the gods—and he
turned back. And he died, soon after."

"Oh, God!" cried Leif. "What is there here either to
damn or to bless?"

Freydis,
Seemingly lost in some thought of her own, appeared
not to hear him; and moments later,
After he had left her there and returned with Gudrid, she
sat in a trance of sunlight in the still room,
Yet as though she were trying to fix an elusive dream. Then
as Leif spoke she stood up and glared at Gudrid.

"You are tired, Freydis. Please go with this lady. She'll
take you where you can rest—can lie down and rest."

"This lady?" said Freydis; and anger flared in her eyes
like flame in a black sun.

"Because you ask me," said Gudrid to Leif. "Otherwise
I'd never put hand to hers."

"The hands," he said,
"Are no longer those you think, for she does not know them."

"This lady I know," said Freydis.
"I didn't come here to see her or to hear her insults."

"Please go with her, Freydis. She'll lead you."

"She'd lead me to hell if she could. I haven't forgotten
how I followed her once. It was wilderness,
Dark—dark—a deep forest of darkness. Her hair shining,
a helmet of gold in the twisting ways

No paths. We kept slashing and breaking a path. I was
   torn bloody that time! I was lost!
And always this silent vigil walking ahead. And the tangle
   of vines. And the steep glare of the sand
Somewhere we came to. I was hungry and thirsty—oh,
   famished. And I was alone. Oh, no—
I followed her once. Oh, no! Leif! Leif! Oh, no!
   Leif! Let me go!"

                    The light
Shuddered with blue shadow and going; and Leif in a while
   came alone out of his house to the new cairn.
"Ah, Tyrker—so lately laid in the good ground. Into
   your grave we broke no weapons
For you bore none. But my grief breaks there, my
   foster-father, my teacher and wise friend.
Tell me Gudrid was wrong: that the land was not evil.
   Hard is it on earth,
Ax-time and sword-time, and men at each other's throats
   to slay and to hold
What holds them after all. Swordless you wandered in
   groves of Vinland and found there
The ripe grapes of your childhood and wore them for
   crown and drank of the wine,
And were happy and fell asleep. O, long and quiet,
   dreamless, untortured sleep!

"Did we find more than we were meant to find? Come
   by long westward sailing
Where we were never meant to go, since we could not
   stay? Once having walked that land
We knew all others harsher. And though it could not
   be ours we set names on its shores
And marked it with some of our dearest bones; but we knew
   all the same it was not evil.
Only that it was not ours, only that it waited."

And the twilight
Filmed the last fiery pulse of the beating air and closed
    upon the sea and the sky
And Leif still standing by the cairn of Tyrker and staring
    into the blackening night. Below him
The drums of the waves thudded deeper under the night.
    Where ocean and sky join
Darkness had hidden the line, and all the way. Yet
    beyond that—long leagues beyond—
He watched through his closed eyes the shining beaches
    rising in salt-dazzle air
As though freshly thrust glistening out of the waves;
    and heard the leaves in the wind, the rustle of meadows.
Beyond Götterdämmerung, Wonderstrand: the bright dunes
    lifting from the tide-rim;
And that same sea which throbbed darkly here
There flooding forward in a wide dance—loosed, surf-slung,
    flanged with sunlight—in praise to the land.

SCRIMSHAW (1959)

Come Green Again

If what heals can bless
Can what blesses heal?
And all come green again
That was bodied forth
Years and years ago?
Years before my time.

Yet things I deepest learned
Turn into memory
As though no man's creation
But enlarges mine;
As though no man's existence
But was also mine
In its lonesomeness.

Henry Thoreau bent
In his boat on Walden Pond
Whistling his wooden flute
Under midnight stars
Across the stars in the water.

Hawthorne and Melville parting
At night in Liverpool,
Parting on a rainy corner
For the final time,
Something unsaid between them.

Mark Twain in moonlight
Standing in his Hartford house,

That wounded, beautiful man,
His hands at his white hair
While he sang "Nobody knows
The troubles I see but Jesus."

Then in broad daylight
The ladies of Camden drawing
Their skirts and kids aside
To avoid the dirty man
As Whitman hobbled past,
His basket on his arm
Filled with his book for sale.

Can such existences
Help but heal our hearts
Or such lonesomeness
Help but bless in us
That everlasting change
Which is our changelessness
And our humbleness?
And all come green again.

What I have learned enough
To have as air to breathe
Returns as memory
Of undiminished love:
That no man's creation
But enlarges me.
O all come green again.

All Memory

The trees smoke with fog.
Old ghosts around me.
After the rain spoke warm air, cold ground,
Slow, coastal wind,
Woke these, but not to walk;
To talk what I recall.

Stand stiff in their stirring robes
Like that host of men in my dream
Who stared blind and silent
Toward the shuttered sea;
And now surround me.
Hooded, faceless, listening.

O ghosts, stay round me!
Soft is this guttural utterance
Of spring. And the mutter
Of the rain renewed in fog
Darkens. Unlost, all memory
Subsides to this stillness.

The Difference

The buffalo loomed at the far loop of the field:
Though mildly grazing in twilight, a thunderhead tethered.
Spectators—man and two children—some others—
Clutched tickets and kept their distance, regarding the rare beast.

271

We were—after all—suddenly there—there in the same grass
At the edge of our town: the familiar vacant lot
Usurped by the savage shape which grazed inattentive:
We grew—embarrassed, frightened—into shy invaders.

Staring and silent, we stood back. Though the crickets rang
And the evening star opened low over the western fence
The shadowy field was bisontine; the ground shook—
Once—with the thud of an absent-minded forefoot.

The little girl said to her father "I want to go see him";
But the boy dared not: he watched them hand in hand
Go slowly within the dusk to confront—quite close—
While he stayed alone among strangers—that hunching darkness.

Silhouette now: the buffalo: horned ghost
Of an ancient philosopher, bearded and ominous,
Transmigrated, neither free nor dead. Nothing occurred
To the father and sister. They returned safe. The three went home.

Wax

A covey of cotton-dressed, apple-breasted girls
Squealed from the hut as the two boys crossed the field
And were gone when the boys reached the hut,
Entered and saw the wax thing on the floor.

Not a candle. By projecting themselves
Immensely (so it seemed to them) older,
The boys knew—there in the damp shadows
Of musty ruins—what the replica was.

Glans end hung broken on the central string.
Half as thick as their wrists the thing made
A frightening excitement when their thin fingers
Explored the hard rod of dirty yellow.

They hid it under a rotted floorboard,
Not knowing why they hid it, any more
Than they imagined why, unlike themselves,
The girls had not merely touched for future luck.

Merrill's Brook

Sun over all and air over all and clover
Ripens with bees the summer afternoon
Where pasture right angles at the slanted oak
And swirls the narrow brook to a round brown pool.

The banks are skin-shiny with twenty boys
That flicker warm light into the shade and out,
Running. They leap to a hang of rope and swing
Above the water, let go with a shouting plunge.

The larger and skillful revolve their bald behinds
On a wheel of headover diving, and here jounce
Beginners flouncing, one foot careful in shallows,
Dog-paddlers, and ankle-deep a little brother

Who stands blondly glistening, unspoken-to.
One anxious mongrel circles among the bathers
Who jump back and forth, amphibious of June:
The air's white-knived with knees and shoulder-blades.

Or loll in grass; and now and then pair off
To hide in alder thickets with hot hands,
Emerging red to dive—the hurried thud
Of racing bare-soled on bluet-bevelled earth.

So on so on a hundred summer days
Till the stranger, the stout and hairy Adam, came
With soap and a pleading smile and called to us
While we scrambled to clothes and ran and ran away.

The Ghost

Beyond grown taller pines there's the same house.
Below the house the pond, shrunken by drought,
Is pocked with red and yellow leaves. The silence
Webs from the locked doors and curtained windows,
The stilled pond, the weeds where gardens were,
My hesitance to speak what I do not know,
And failure of anticipated ghosts.
The absent strangers who possess this house
Are nearer, being unknown, than my lost friends.
Intruder on today, I see no summer
Fleshed with naked bodies at the shore,
Nor hear on the cold terrace liquored laughter.
Under its corner draught a clutch of leaves
Circles like wounded bats scratching the stones.
A disused theater, expectant of others
Who needn't care, for there's no mark of us.
My friend the architect of this house is dead,
Those who loved and built, divorced, dispersed,
The Pan-pipes child changed to a man somewhere.
So, what I came for is not here, and it

Departs with me who hoped one revenant
And fetched the wind spiralling in my ribs
And pallor of clouding sun thin through my hands.

Dead Leaves Out of Place

If I return to walk these woods
It is to walk a memoir of desire
Along the lake shore and the hill of pine,
November noon; waters in a pallid sun,
Hillslope under the pine strewn
With a sift of beech leaves, blown from
Some other hill, here strange and the pine
Made strange; blink of a cold day.

Grayed at the rocky edge the lake's seulette
Lips the wind; it is a thinned way
I return amidst promise of ice and
Some recollection as of an illness
Making the place important:
Adolescent delirium, joy and terror,
Lust's invention and the real fever—
Tremor of sun over these dry-bright leaves.

I remember the girl, as one
Reminded of his forgotten poem
Blushes for fabrication, yet may be
By history touched a little; retrospective love
Fulfills itself with a later stranger—
Requires the stilled woods, the skinned mirror,
Knowledge that wherever they belong
Leaves like these return to live again.

Chapter Two

Listen—I'll say you a
Park in the city, a
Park in the dusk just
As the snow is beginning:
The gray-blue, the sweet-cold, the
Whispering rustling.
                              And
—Do you remember?—
Floor by floor the lights rising
As darkness filled up
The tall wells of the streets
Gigantically ringing the
Small empty park where
The thin snow slid in
As if it would fall
Through the dusk there forever,
Amidst gears', horns' wrangles
Hushing a circle;
The gray-white, the sweet cold.
                              Oh

—Now you remember—
How young and unhappy and
Lovely you were
How uselessly in
Love we were; and there
Walking alone in New York in the snow
You had nobody anywhere to see to
Talk to nowhere to go.

276

Summer Place

I think of that summer place where the catalpa flowers
    were chock with sun,
Tree-full, leaf-lifted over the low roof until they were
    stormed to the grass;
They lay like a spendthrift of gnomish orchids surfed from
    a world too small for us to see.

We walked on them. We observed in a day their brown-vein
    stain. Shriveled, they were gone soon
With all such flakes of light that make May and June so far
    from bean-stretching August
Wherein we can better remember—do begin to remember—
    October, December, can never June or May.

We were young then. Summer did not go by—it stood huge
    on the house and in the fields
As if, despite our remembrance, an unbudgeable heat held us;
    and in water-scented nights
For its brief relenting we danced our stripped-down dances
    beneath the black plaques of the tree.

But it did go. Fall flew us away. We were confused with
    seasons, are chilled by so many years.
I imagine the house now as I never saw it at all: stark in
    leafless light and weathered shutters locked,
The crackling sound of someone walking across the crinkled
    pods strewn on the ground.

In That House Where Day Was Night

for W. H. Gerry

Now the old dream comes again.
The stone house in streaming rain
Beyond rain-thickened trees, beyond
Wet-dark wall and the blinded pond;
And I the unseen man shut in.

So my day-dream comes again
And as if time had stopped. No less
That I would not believe or bless
Rained-out sun and the clock locked
In a perpetual usufruct
Which, breathless that I breathed upon,
Left me both living and alone.

Yet the dream grows; the tempest gust
Wild on the roof where I am housed
Safe and sure and safe and sure.
The utmost tree roots can endure
Chaining the wrathful writhe of trees,
Thunder exploding in the chimneys
And the blank endless roar of rain
Upon the cannoned ground—their strain
Proves all my peace and certitude,
Their war my wall.

                    But for what good
Strides like a stranger in the dream

My friend who died? But now I seem
To remember he believed in rain—
Days of his living communication—
Also that he would break death down
And speak through ashes under stone.
"Cary! Cary!" I call; but pale,
Smiling, cheerfully wistful still,
Across the woods he walks and blurs.
The chilled rain on my face answers.
I close the door for my disbelief
As I had opened it for grief,
And turn away.

        The day-dream has
Become a whirl of silences,
Vortex of blacked-out memories.
I cannot say *When was I? Who was
I? am I?*—Where are they gone
Who knew my name? And with a long
Cloud-driven crash the storm attacks
The stone house, and the house cracks
Open to the cracked-open night,
Wind flecking the trees with starlight.

Stars weave among each other over
The windy woods, and I remember
"Nothing that sounded once is lost."
Voices of living man and ghost
Arriving on the withering air
Expand the welkin where they are,
And move and are, and recklessly
Dissolve and die, arise and die,
Re-form in coldest night, rehearse
The unbraiding and braiding universe.

Point of View

for George Loveridge

The man on the roof, his back against the chimney,
Spies as unseen as though he were not there,
Or had been there a quarter-century;
                                    anyway, evening
Starts to come up the street, whispering first
In the bicycle wheels of the boy who lights the lamps
Who whistles from corner to corner, diminuendo—
Gone under the stride of Baby Shea
On whose policing bulk the bluish light
Flat-foots the shadowy concrete. There's a hint of mist.

The sky shifts altogether west now, drops for all
But Mr. Pitman. His incessant cane
Knocks and knocks the pavement and where he climbs
By counted steps safe to his memorized door.
The lamp his little hunch-backed sister lights
Smoulders a medicine that lets him breathe.
The wall closes and evening seems to pause.

Around the corner comes Mr. McGillicuddy,
But blind-drunk only, and down on his knees he flops
Fumbling at the picket gate, calling his daughters.
"Ah," shouts the unseen man against the chimney,
"McGillicuddy, it's always the way this hour:
You think it's the old gate of your childhood home
And misremember the latch. It's the other side."
But nobody hears him, and the favorite daughter
Lugs the old man in.

                    Sighing the twilight blurs
Arrival of Mr. Barker in the side street,
Hurrying late from the hardware shop to home
Hidden in snowball bushes behind the hedge.
Presently he will stuff the kitchen doors
With all the repetitive read-out newspapers,
Turn on the unilluminating gas
And lie down patiently. But Mrs. Barker
With usual competence will arrive home too early.

In the gray-shingled house to eastward, death
Has just occurred to Toshie Weaver's mother.
Black-gloved, his plump and middle-ageing hands
Project a moment in the helpless dusk
And creak the shutters closed.

                            Looking up,
Looking like Mark Twain, old Mr. Kaull
Clatters tin watering-can on the slate stoop,
And to the man above him by the chimney
The air around that beautiful white head
Spouts with a magic trick of Audubon cards,
Gifts of his kindness, fixed and singing birds
Which never need perch on Murphy's forbidden trees
High-fenced above Kaull's garden, but will ring
This childish air, bright even in rising fog,
Between the schoolhouse and the harbor horns.

Through the chimney Mrs. Sharwell's voice
Feebly reciting Mary Baker Eddy
Reedily conjures up another room
Into which, it says, she soon will gladly pass.
Clamor of two children resisting bedtime
Sounds from the second floor and then subsides.
And now it is nearly dark.

                    The corner street-light
Grows taller and keeps humming to itself.
Two backyards to the north the night whirls spiced
With Captain Pearson's peonies; though which
Are pink and which are white—
                              but now between
This yard and that the foggy scarves float up
Fragrance of the Wilbars' clematis,
A drenching sweetness where a woman walks
Straight-backed the gray-brick path, across the lawn,
And roves from fence to fence, gripping the four,
Confirmed that all are stout as they were made
So long ago. She glances toward the chimney
Of the next roof, and as she turns away
And fades absorbed in darkness, fireflies
Spatter softly before her where she moves
And float a traveling glimmer at her feet
Over the hidden grass.

                       And now the night
Shuts down with fog, and all the houses drift
As in a tide that sinks them under the sea.

Friday So Soon

There were many people on the island
Though, looking back at it now, it seems we were
Mostly alone together; we were allowed
The customary two weeks; the first
Floated like a slowed dream, like those boats
Windless and weightless and mirrored
Within folded lusters of air. The sea—

It is strange how at once on the island
You forget sea as the way of travel: others'
Continual arrival and disappearance
Enclosed us—safely, we thought, while
The sea-way which bore and must take us
Became God's moat to keep us.
We played in and out of it repeatedly.
Along shore that grass we almost sank in.
Weather spiralled from the full moon: storm
Shot rain and spray in salt horizontals
Three days. There was that too. Yet afterwards
The evening star like a pinwheel nail
Set all the galaxies awhirl until
Our island spun among them—
And then the sun with its wide quietness
Covered the sky and sea. The last days
Grew tense with being last: for instance,
Time and desire for swimming nearly vanished. We
Looked from sea at the grass and trees and flowers.
We were stilled by a recollected plan.
Sometimes I think I must have imagined it all
And yet how real you seemed when we ran with the sea.

Memento

Bessie Townley Scott, 1885-1952

1

This is a rocksaw seacoast.
Puddingstone lugs the thud of glacial death.
Nevertheless the thin earth of the clifftops

Hedges with wild roses the summer sea,
And I say this headland is for us forever
The sheriff of the morning star.

Far down there are cave-cuts where high tide
Jets a commotion of foam.
The sterile wear is slow is
A spoon of pearled emerald from a hundred years.
Yet eastward at evening the ocean
Takes credit for the moon.

Cow-sound foreign there our bell-buoy gonged
Tins and tans; off Brenton Reef
Our lightship makes a medallion.
We have chained these things and now
Would see them only if they disappeared.
We are if we touch the waters a skirl of snow.

Though I have seen navies, vicious though ours,
Soundless past these islands, out of this bay,
Curve toward Gibraltar;
I have imagined dragon-headed ships
Arriving here ten centuries out of port
Loom in marine erasure of history.

Cantilevered into surf this coast
Juts nonhuman; graves of shipwrecked were
Hurricane-gouged; but the swallows
Fly in and out of the earth, fly through
Plunges of gulls that rise
White, shadowed, and white in the dulcet sun.

And I say of these weathers I choose
A seamless afternoon—mansion of glass
As huge as childhood—sea and sky: I say

For an ancient anchor grass-grown
This wreath of roses between stone and salt air
Is breath of the dead whose memories now are mine.

2

Will you hear that I spoke these stones and trees,
These stones under trees, trees over the houses,
These streets and walks, these dooryards hedged and fenced
In the old way, this little town?

I say, without my voice this is all lost, it is nothing.
But I am the passionate marriage of memory and love
And which of you knows even my name or my voice?
How could you know today is today having forgotten
Yesterday and tomorrow.
                              Yet—whether
You hear or know—I speak; I say that here
Night pours westward off the back of the world
And the sea pours out the sun which rising
Shafts with its tiers of escalators
The moist streets of the morning;
                              and the streets
Fill with fathers, skip with schoolchildren,
They hush for cool cobbledy sound of horse and wagon
Somewhere around the corner and coming nearer;
They are lanes between lines of washing hung to dance
Over mothers and babies and sandboxes till noon.
Till I say *Sleep*. It is three o'clock. The sun
Inaccessible hovers a while stilled.
No footsteps—no door—no doorbell—all is emptied.
I alone stand, a fixed dream, and watch
That piazza opening through its leafless vines
And the wind in the rockingchair.

This lady's memory of these things is gone.
Of us and sixty-seven years her knowledge
Is gone. While you stare down at her long-loved face
The nonexistence which shakes you is your own.

Now you have come to stare at the statue of death
Its terror is in your recognition of it and,
Unlike a real statue, its failure to change,
Its inability to respond. And this conceived you.

From what you know, from what you can bear to see
This must be buried soon. And only for you
Now and always light is everywhere altered,
All the colors of the world are otherwise.

Whom do the mourners see? A girl—a ghost—
A bride—an old and tired lady—a stranger?
They pause and make her momentary replica.
Whom do the mourners see? Themselves. Themselves.

As wave into wave, so memory into memory
Folds, falls forward, follows till some far
And unimaginable coast receives forever
The final landfall of oblivion.

You remember fright and agony were here
But pain cannot be posthumous for her.
The burial signal is thunder and rain. Say *Sleep*.
Sleep, lady: no longer remember even me.

4

Psyche whose threnodic hands
Wash the winter darkness white
Move between the stars and starlight
Where the worlds are whirled to sands
Where all music disappears,
All the answers which we know
Less than shadow less than echo,
The emolument of tears
Turned immaculate fall of snow
Turned anonymous design
Strict as stars that as they fell
Fell unrecognizable,
Now no longer think to tell
Which were hers and which were mine,
Now no further realize—
Psyche whose threnodic hands
Heal the cicatrice of years—
What had soothed her hands and eyes.
Move between the sun and sunrise.

5

Again and yet again midsummer night
Hangs the prismatic curtains of the moon
Draping as with stilled and visible winds
The ocean's quietly dancing arches, leaping
Point Judith to Brenton Reef and to Sakonnet
And sweeping past Aquidneck's phosphorent roofs
Stands in this lifting light on the great bay
And all its shadowy islands: Conanicut,
Gould and Rose and north to Coddington Cove
The twisted whale of Prudence Island—fixed
As in a mindless memory of love.

The moonlight seems to shudder. It is the sea's
Intermittent pausing pulse, its flicker
Of nerves, that shudder. And even these remote
As a sleeping face watched dimly in a mirror;
Watched carefully as though it might awaken
Although I know it will only disappear
And the emptied glass swirl to bluish fog
Quick to be lost in the moon's nameless color.
Although I think that deep within these waters
Stares the figurehead of a nameless lady
Whose long farewells speak from her lidless eyes.

Now this wide glass of sea is voyageless.
The lightship blinks for nothing. The bell-buoy
Bangs for danger of emptiness and home.
At the cliffbase the tide is a caress,
Neither impersonal nor aggressive now
But in an alien armistice feigning peace.
This headland now embodied by the dead
Moves in the kinship of the moon which is
A memory of light and which is love,
And gifted with roses' wild recurrent grace
Sets forth toward day on the rugosen sea.

The Last One

Now all that name are gone:
Friends and relatives
Summoned—but left to come
Are nurses, acquaintances.

This neutral ground opened
To be engaged as grave

Arrests the fatiguing air
Which only strangers breathe.

In ninety years she suffered
All other graves nearby:
Now joins them unattended
By lives of memory.

Though undisturbed by her
And the unrequested flowers,
Her long-experienced dead
Reciprocally cease.

Into the Wind

The child grabbed my hand and made me run with him
Under the slate-dark sky in air chill with grape.

So much November night came rushing toward us
From all four quarters while he danced and sang
As if for a spring morning, and while he ran
A so determined undirected way, I was amazed
To hear him ask where we were going, and could only say
Just before I lost him, "Not all the way together."

I heard his diminishing steps and then the wind.

Then the clouds commenced shifting arrangements of light
Of the cold and mensal, unmentionable moon.

Two Lives and Others

Beyond the field where crows cawed at a hawk
The road bent down between oaks, pines, and maples,
Maples skimming the air with terra cotta.
The oaks spat acorns over scurries of squirrels.
Moss crunched stiff underfoot, and overhead
The sky was freezing gradually, white across blue.
We hurried our walk through shadows, yet it was
A noticeable sort of afternoon:
We honored a faded robin and considered
The importance of the color gray on bluejays.
A woodchuck, all an urgent clumsiness,
Made his tumbling run, then he saw us,
Plunged, hid, and screamed his whistle of fear.
Round the next bend to twilight we went past
A solitary house, one room lamplighted,
An old man at supper alone facing the wall.
If he was aware of us he gave no sign.
We circled home, that last day before snow.

The Mother

Bowed down she turned but, halfway up the stairs,
Broke over—fingers, gray head, on the banister.
She cried out: "Everyone I met today
Had someone to take care of them but me.
Everyone wishing me a Merry Christmas,

Then I come home to this dark and empty house.
Aren't you two children grown enough by now
To know what it's been to bring you up alone,
Earn every cent it took? And you don't give
A damn to be with me on Christmas Eve."
And we stood frightened there, seeing her cry
For the first time: deserted, shamed to be
Shamed by having not known what we did,
And seared by shame and pity then we cried
For the first time since we were children, and
She hurried down to us and put her hands
On both our shoulders and said "Oh, my dear boys!
What did I do wrong to hurt you so!"

Mrs. Severin

Mrs. Severin came home from the Methodist Encampment,
Climbed naked to the diningroom table and lay down.
She was alone at the time but naturally told of it afterward.
"Lord! Lord!" she had called out. "Thou seest me. Wherein is
    my fault?"

When she heard of it, second-hand, Mrs. Birchfield laughed till
    she cried.
"My God!" she said, "I'd like to've seen her getting up there!"
For Mrs. Severin, you see, was a very stout old lady,
A spilling mass by buttons, shawls, pins and ribboned eyeglasses
    held together.

The eyeglasses were a shift of drama: hoisted for reading aloud,
    lowered for talking;
They were not interrruption. Mrs. Severin's soft incessant sibilance

Through all the days she visited and rocked by the window
Braided inextricably Bible and autobiography. Jesus was near.

"The morning Encampment began the Lord suddenly told me to
    go.
Ran all the way down-street to the cars for Canobie Lake,
Didn't fasten my dress or tie my shoes. Left the house open.
    Young ones at the neighbors.
'Lord,' I said, 'I am thy servant'—and stayed the whole beautiful,
    blessed week."

On the listening child her showers of quotation pattered a
    drugged dream.
" 'Thought becomes word. Word becomes act. Act becomes char-
    acter. Character becomes destiny.'
Remember that. And praise the Lord," she said, giving off also
Odor of camphor, old rose jars and muttonleg sleeves. "Amen!"

The husband long gone who wasted her inheritance; the irritable
    children
Who hated to have to have her now; the friends who took her in
    now and again: gone.
Here in her false hair and handmedowns, patiently talking—
    talking:
Old Mrs. Severin who once, brave on a diningroom table, naked
    confronted her unanswering Lord.

Codicil for Pvt. John Hogg's Will

Gray and blue, the boy ghosts with guns are in the spring woods:
Now—a century after—they are here.
West, the Blue Ridge is a line of march along the sky and
    into the sky—

A memorial—
And those wide miles of fields roll up to it as though with
    love, for the fallacy is always pathetic;
But in these woods, poignant with April, the boys in a mist
    that makes the morning old
Rove in a haunt of spring. One can see why.

Sunshine, thin and young, burning like mirrored light, probes
    the hepatica-broken leaves
And blankets of violets flung to the gray ground
And windless moss furled on the cedars
And the brook living shyly amidst embracing, stumbling,
    fallen trees.
There's bloodwort, brief blossoming.

So youth, one hears, died here long ago.
By the five-toned mourning dove—not only, not alone; no less
Weave of sparrow, waxwing, finch, and cardinal birdsong,
    daylong birdsong,
Riddling, caroling chorus through the slowly opening day.

One, a stranger from among the victors if there are victors,
    can see why
This could be held dearest of all and to be fought for,
Here in the willow way
Dogwood's ivory stairs to nowhere,
The deep flowering judas.

Phelps Putnam

He twirled his tabled highball. Darkening,
The room minced back and forth in shadows and

His glass I noticed was a child's tumbler
Dappled with a painted pony rockered.

I wondered how it came there. "If my heart
Were strong enough to write again," he said.
"But doctors—." Then he shrugged his old-young face
And poured more whisky in my jelly-glass.

"One can be legendary even at forty,"
He said, "but that is to be alive only
In other people's pasts." He lit the lamp
With careful down-adjustment of the wick.

The tall bookcases righted themselves but all
The uncommunicative countryside
Pressed against the blackened windows closer;
As though a vacuum listened. "If I could

Remember," he remarked. "When I was young
Why, all of us were going to be great men."
He let his drink stand by the lamp and thought.
I looked away. "But to recall one's self,"

I heard him say, "—such ruthless appetite."
Projected from the glass the light had made
The painted toy gigantic—shadow of horse
Massive, silent, living, real, on the wall.

Re-Run

I was that dancer. On the screen
Dances again who once was I

Head Grecian-curled and lean, the lean
Pectoral hardness and his hard thigh

Strident across the film in great
Loves of leaping, in whirls, in slow
Erectile pause of weightless weight
Perfected twenty years ago.

They often re-run. I save to sit
And spy upon the youth who had
Youth without its opposite,
Promise therefore that went bad.

See how he dances ignorance
Of childhood and of you and me;
Half-naked, full magnificence,
He spins before a moonlit sea

Whose tones orchestral and perverse
Whisper, snarl on the sound-track;
But all are caught around those terse
Hips and within that stallion back

To stiff finalities of strength
Feet thundering at the horn's cry,
Until the plot extrudes its length
When in the movie he can die.

Celebrity

Take this jeweled hand but do not hold it:
We bear to be touched momentarily if at all.
This palm has held London and Paris once

And this, New York. You that have never had it
Cannot conceive the weariness of triumph,
The unrelinquishable weariness.
There are in the world similar hands—a few;
We avoid meeting; such weight is unmanageable.
You, we perceive, being jeune and intelligent
May in turn perceive our graciousness bends.
The habits of greatness are so swiftly learned
Yet stay unalterable, my dear young man.
Oh yes, we need you. Let us admit we need you
Everywhere momentarily. Be numerous.
But never allude to others' indiscretions
In all those memoirs which insinuate
The sort of bread these hands once broke upon
And what haired thighs these stiffening fingers stroked.
How much we must forget to smile, to sleep!
The more you think you know the less you know,
And even this we have said you have imagined.
We who were young, poor, arrogant, insurgent,
Are—what else can we say?—are old and famous.

William Primrose Gets His Guarnerius

No fiddle of morning:
All the light in it
Is traveled.

Guarnerius Viola
Shaped of a woman's body,
Three centuries,
Burnished maple;
The night tone shining.

Her silence and sleep so long
Webbed beneath strung starlight.

But William,
Barefooted in kilts to school,
Kind-fathered past jungles of billboards,
Believing in the resurrection,
Traveled humbly toward her,
Grew into the dark forest, the night tone,
Wordless with music.

Now his face bends upon her,
His bow and fingers move:
From interference of learned mortal love
Across far-traveled light
All hymns arise and sing
Human and deathless.

To awaken this
Required
No ordinary prince.

Frieda 75

> *She opened her eyes, and green*
> *They shone, clear like flowers undone*
> *For the first time, now for the first time seen.*
>
> —D. H. Lawrence

Frieda is the old grandma in the fairy tale
In her magic house deep in the German woods.
Why is her house magic? Frieda lives there.

She bends over pots and pans, stirring and tasting
Wonderful broths for all the children who come.

Listen, she laughs like bells all over the room.
That is because there are tears in the broth she stirs.
She traveled a far way to arrive at her house,
Of course leaving much behind her, and learned about tears.
Drink what she has and you'll tell the truth forever.

Like any nice white-haired grandma in the world
She will trot out her jewelbox and show you things:
A necklace and maybe a huge ring from Lorenzo.
What Frieda really wears are a man's words.
That's the magic. She opens her eyes and green they shine.

Just Before the Hurricane

Said the old woman to the young woman, "Darlin,
Are ye a whisky drinker? I am myself.
It helps me keep this fist doubled and ready.
Ah, it's pull your punches and no fights for art,"
Said the old woman under her sag of hair.

Said the old woman, "Now it's nobody hurt.
But what in the name of God is poetry for?
I'll have ye know we've sunk to a truthless lot.
I'd scorn to damp my feet in this tadpole pond,"
Said the wild old woman who was never bewildered.

Said the old woman, "Don't forget I knew
That giant among all the men of my youth.
And knew the beauty queen who tramped his heart.

But it was me—never her—understood his poems,"
Said the old woman angry with the world.

Said the old woman, slugging herself again,
" 'More geese than swans now live, more fools than wise.'
An Elizabethan sang that stave for us.
My time was all guts and brains and I've outlived it,"
Said the old woman shaking her bottle at the flooding wind.

Paging Mr. Paterson

for William Carlos Williams

On this day I was born
Forty-eight years ago.
And what's it to you? or me?

I sit in a little house.
I can see on the sun outside
Apricot blossoming white
And the pink-blossoming peach
In cold mountain air.
I have come this far, this high,
From the slow hill of birth.

I have read the morning away
With an old man's youngest poem
Made in his seventy-fifth year—
A time when all is one—
To say that virgin and whore
Are as one, and Art is all:
The poem become at last

A vast meadow of flowers,
A brave dance of Yes.

That old man, mad for words.

I recall the day I said
"I am twelve! I am twelve! I am twelve!"
That day I knew I was twelve.
Who knows now what I am?
Or how far I have come?
But closer to this hawk-high sun.

I should like to send these trees,
White and pink over black,
To the old man, to say
"Here, these are all for you."
And: "Neither you nor I
Are in the habit of prayer;
So will you *wish* me then
For the year I am seventy-five
The meadow, the measured dance."

I watch the flowered branches.
They curve to my one desire.
They bend toward my last desire.

The Man at Mid-Century

We cannot guess how long he'll wait.
He paces in his room alone
Imagining someone must come
Whose voice will force the lag of fate.
He paces puzzled, helpless, dumb,

Or sits beside the telephone
Hoping it may ring his ring
And someone solve him everything.
Television, radio:
Sessions to watch and listen to
Lest someone there let slip the clue
Of what he needs to need to know.
All possibilities allowed,
He leaves the latchkeys in his locks
And walks among the city crowd
Seeking the face that will reveal
Someone whose quickening answers frame
His inarticulate questioning.
He hurries home to letter-box,
To rooms as empty, to the same
Expectancy of dreams and drink.
Pacing he waits for me or you
Or anyone to speak his name:
Someone to tell him what to do
Someone to tell him what to think
Someone to tell him what to feel

Unfurnished Room

You stand alone in an emptied house
And stare from the sill into a vacant room:
Wallpaper whirls around the gaping closet.
The six-over-six windows to the east
Are reproduced at slant across the floor.
So this is morning, of a clear day.
Your heart, the only sound, accelerates
Because nothing yet has happened to you here
Or everything has happened and is over.

Two

There was that fall the fall of desire
And in the senseless night a sense of wires
Cut, plugs pulled from the darkened switchboard;
And then the silent cold like unspoken words,
And then the snow silencing depths and heights.
Together we walked alone the white-twigged night
Followed by our desperate, disparate tracks
Which even to us were lost when we looked back.

The Wrong Is Mixed

Can cockcrow fix a landscape?
Morning anywhere in the world.
Country nostalgias. Here is
Season of spiders, webs before wind.
Blue air curved yellow with fruit,
Green disintegrates: decomposition
Is peaceful. Dove wings rising
Clap an applause of peace.
At early crow, light's a long level.

We hear that the world will end;
What heart believes it? We hear of
Beginningless and endless universe;
What mind imagines it? And if
We are unwebbed and the wind comes

302

That blows the world away, betrayed
From green for the last time—cockcrow
Must cry up that tearing air like
Memory of the morning of the world.

Here on water, one scarlet leaf for love.

What I Assembled and Dissemble

What I assembled and dissemble
Mix and merge in this bird-drenched wood.
What I invent and what remember
Will never save me from the sod.

Those held loving and those abandoned
Sigh together when I am gone.
Under the grass is understanding:
Ash in a jar, *I-told-you-so.*

Every lilac that blossomed is
In this one flower—take it for yours.
Such fragrance gives so brief a blessing
That all my Mays come back in tears.

Surf of wind on the willow-walk,
This fluttering shuttle of flying song,
Mean what the cherry's white floating fall
Means to morning: We knew this once.

We are deep tranced in repetition
Having ourselves the frailest sum—
Forgetting, forever young in passion,
How useless is the lie of rhyme.

The Hour Is Late

It seemed to me in the night
I had no art after all.
That all I had tried to make
Was never for its own sake,
Stank with impurity,
And that what my enemies said
My kind friends left unsaid.
Then it seemed to me
I stumbled in a dark hall
In an unfamiliar house
Where I had no business to be.

Did vanity espouse
Such self-deceiving as mine?
As though not tree but vine—
As though not girl but kiss—
Were the reality.
Or had I at first some reason?
The beginning as true for me
As for some luckier men
Who quarried the light of day
Out of such night as this?

There was nothing to which to pray,
And the night was very late.
I could neither love nor hate
Who had lived so long alone
With an invented ghost

That now was utterly gone.
A naked man in a strange house
In the dark, nameless and lost.

The Long Party

Identification had to be by mask.
The party went on so long. So long.
Nobody bared a face. All those lanterns.
It was maggot-time in the blood trees. Even
Above the sludge of the sea that other sound
Ate among us in crepitant whispers.
A few desperate errors aside, there were
No real connections; woman with woman,
Man with man; relief was agitating.
"I am too old to dance," said an old man:
"Will you dance for me?" To somebody young.
I'd have sworn nobody was there. Dark.
Hopefully: "Old people for contrast at a party.
But there's no such thing," he said, "as a hundred years."
In the dusk the children sat discussing death.
Later they were gone—too late—to bed.
A wilder surf of music. That—I thought—
First sounded in a skull two-hands-sized,
Now it roves the sky. But these were maskers
Knew how to dance without hearing the music.
Where the children had hidden I stumbled
Scattering a pattern of letter-blocks
Though in that light I doubt I could have read.
The lawn sloped down to the blue hydrangeas,
The blue hydrangeas held the sea. Apart,
I found a clump of laurel I remembered:
But shriveled. I had dreamed that laurel tall.

The Fall

The stilted beetle steps
Through the leaf-muddled grass.
Branch by branch, yellow
Stains down the poplar trees.

The dusty spiders slink
Into the house. The wind
Sleets across windowpanes
The lilacs' blackened leaves.

In erosion's work
We hide the name of love,
And remember rain
Down the strangers' streets.

No grief is annual.
We smell our blackened hearts
Unseasonably hurt
With their unflaking char.

Foul weather was fair
For poetry and love.
Now without prizes—
As most dogs do—we live.

The old men arrive
Who have the world in charge
And are about to leave.
They toss it carelessly

To the moon and back.
Perhaps. In carelessness
Born of a surety
Fire is posthumous.

We know now that our tears
Are always for ourselves.
We stomp the spiders flat.
The beetle chill's unfelt.

All our news is death.
Clowns are dangerous.
We have proved paradise
The illusion of our eyes.

Watch Hill

Unsexed by the cold sea, prone out of it on the beach,
Too diminished for art, I yet resolving
To write only of seasons other than the present,
To try the imagination, the larger love;
All the while the sanded wind blew over me.

Next-naked the young woman on her back
Slept brown and gold along a blue blanket,
Her children near; I spied upon her thighs
Forked open and the mount of glossy ribs and
All the while the sanded wind blew over her.

Two children small and gold who bucketed,
Built and bashed at variance, and now
Trotted with new knees to borrow some ocean,

Then peered to find if their mother still slept;
All the while the sanded wind blew past them.

Strangers, we three shared an altering patience;
I at my distance beginning to fondle a daydream
On that upturned, abandoned face, and they
Running in close to see when it would claim them,
All the while the sanded wind blew past it.

Their play dropped, sudden as fright among birds
They pounced, calling, shaking and waking her;
I closed my eyes upon her; the plunge and plunge
Of stroking ocean remotely hot and swollen,
And all the while the sanded wind blew between us.

Blue Sleigh

Blue sleigh that fifty winters gone
Swan-breasted heavier snows than ours,
Arrested on your summer lawn
Stands filled with earth and planted flowers.

Its shafts slant empty to the ground
As if they'd never held a horse;
Its runners make the breathless sound
Allotted rust and ghosts, of course.

The flowers are white geranium.
Stuck in June grass it looks as though
Somehow the sleigh had tunneled home
Through one immortal drift of snow.

Present preservative of past?
That what it raced through it contains?
But your illusion will not last:
Here's white geranium and it stains.

You lover of the incongruous:
Better to have your blue sleigh drawn
Through all those daisy fields across
The hills to time's malignant sun.

Exercise in Aesthetics

The lilac bushes were small with winter.
Rain-repeated, the abacus of barberries
Ran red, ran red above the smoking snow
And the green chickweed where it winked.
Low to the ground, fog hovered and blew and shifted.
The house we passed was three miles from the last
And, as it turned out, three miles from the next.
A back road between cold-blackened pines
On a cellar of a morning near December's end.
Nobody visible at the house. My question was
Whom were all the Christmas signals for—
The candles in the windows and the doorwreath
Ribboned to render hemlock a gay creation?
At most a stranger or two passed once a day,
Like us, in a moment passing. For us, then?
Yes, if we happened by. But of necessity
First for the mingled joy of decoration
And whoever made it. How else could it be?

The Double Tree

I do not know why. It is not only
In the April sun the flowered apricot tree—
It is more the shadow of the tree against the wall
The shadow of flowered branches that sets the tree
There in the April sun and on the earth,
Fan coral within the soft sea of spring.
Sparrow and the shadow of sparrow fly
Into the double tree, create it there
So dimensional it must be believed.
What sun objectifies, like us, is real
For this little while in the sun's season.

Love and a Season

Over what freshets of light on April mornings
Robins burble their six-note seesaw-song—
Elm-high above blue damp shadows and valley mist
A prestidigitation, a fountained waste
Of juggled gold that only May will match
With dandelion fields' prodigal silence
Beyond the spume of May.
                              And now farewell
To the June town of ladies in cotton lilac
Bending their frail look upon picketed iris
In hopelessly joined grids of scented yards
That give on the valley view that gives on graves

Tucked in the north corner of the sky. Farewell
That little way down hill to the terraced stillness
Where mosspink stitches the anonymous scars
To a brave indifference of forgetfulness
Under this music thinned and long familiar
Which is not yet exactly mine, for the grave—transfixed,
Oh, my loved ghost!—most mine is not among these
And the house I have to go home to is a new house.

Obdurate Change

Leaves falling falling in the woods
Make a rainy sound across the sun.

All sift and wavering of leaves and shift
Of light—the woods opening everywhere.

Have we names now, walking alone together,
So far from everyone, as two together?

No leaf is the same for any other's eye:
No name is the same, even for you and me.

Leaves falling falling in the woods.
Sun on so many names, the names on stones.

And the stones changing in the mutable air,
Planes of light sliding, melting, re-forming.

The woods walk through us season over season.
Walking their leaves we make the sound of fall.

From Chirico to Charon

Vacancies of Chirico Square repeated as far as Charon's River;
The River invisible from here.
Stone line of the houses empty also; staring, he somehow knew;
By, perhaps, a buttressing vibrance hollowing noon to an unreal
    moonlight,
Zero parthenogenesis ordered inevitably;
And a pack of dry leaves, squeaking wind-driven, crossing the
    road like rats.

To walk inward—to begin to diminish; and he began; slowly.

By the moving assumed the strength, made of a braid of his
    weaknesses,
And his discovery of this; as he changed, gospels occurred and
    were birds around him
And he continued steadily and unhindered;
In his progress was his living, and its direction certain
Now he accomplished the one defense against general disaster:
    imagined his death.

Vanished beyond the Square he arrived at the River;
Of the coin of his life he could not tell the value, but rejoiced
    at the light weight of it in his mouth.

N. M.

Walking over the loma and down to the arroyo
In the windy weather of the year the time the world

Melts to spring and here dries thin in the smashing sun,
I might have descended cliffs of the moon to an old sea floor.

And parasitical suck in the cedars like green sea-sponge
Flecked pink, emblem of kisses, polyp-building, coral-
Budding, mistletoe writhed to its skeletal achievement.
I saw on the sand two lovers knotting their naked sprawl.

I saw moving steadily, earth into sky, like the conjugal
Hyphen a single plane bagged heavy with seed of death.
Amongst these and upright with my choice I chose
Where to be lonely to learn to tell mountains from clouds.

Between Ironwood and the Sea

The sand around the ironwood
And the ironwood remain an alien place.
Though I have watched remotest land
Close in snow to a remembered field
This goes, like dreams slept out.
Daylight is the world.

Buckhorn twists in the lilac shoots.
Where last year's oak leaves lock
There is the prickly pear.
Against the adobe wall
Hollyhocks sway with bees.
And then the rain punctual upon dust
Becomes nostalgic acid on the tongue,
Then lids the day and fills the air
With dark and lilac-loaded cold.

Black mesa and the Merrimack
Adjacent in the darkened dream
Split in the daylight world
Till each man move between
Salt womb and ironwood
Sea and desert, the breathless places.
Only between them marriage happens.

Here in the youngest land
Whose yucca roots in rock, whose rock
Is a rage of fire stilled to iron,
We walk that earth where the sea
Most lately was.
Here in stone is the backbone of a fish
Here the rendered fern:
The difference within the resemblances
Holds all our art and joy and grief.

On hard clay shaped ten hundred years
By the bare tread of the nerved foot,
I saw the old men who used to dance
Chanting and drumming for the virile dancers
Who were aped by children
Wavering in evergreens;
And the possible sanity of life
Seemed the very sun over them,
And I who could never dance for it
Wept for joy.

Everything sifts from the human hand
Like dust, like water.
A mix of the two can be shaped
And reshaped in sameness with a difference forever.
Look! I had been told

There could be snow on the blossoming lilac.
I have seen it now and stayed
Because it is so.

The Blue Tree

The leaves fell all from the tree.
The birds flew into it
And made for a while a blue tree.
They were jays—sarah and pinon jays:
Could perch intensely blue
And fly it intenser still:
Out they went as on strings
Circling, clustering in again.
Green the tree had been; then gold—
For days gold; now a moment blue.

Winter was beginning to come.
Snow on the mountains. From houses
All the blue doors in the wind clapped
"Hail Mary! Hail Mary!"
The sun sang like wires everywhere.
I, in another's dream—a strange country
Which belonged to me though not I to it:
I could speak, but got no answers.

If I grow old—I came to know this—
The world I die from can never be
The world most mine. Green given,
Gold from green; but then
The blue, temporary tree.

To love is to stay, and that
Will have been another place and season.
The tree flies green to somebody's other dream.

Light Enough to Go Round

> New perceptions—even light-houses
> Can throw them far inland. . . .
> —Haniel Long

The light that wheels through night
To guide the ships at sea,
One third of its turning light
Seems burning uselessly.

Two thirds of the time it keeps
Its vigil on rocks and waves
But each time round it sweeps
Over houses, fields and graves
Where its light may waken some
Who don't yet sleep too hard.

In necessitous go-and-come
With nothing inland to guard
It abandons indifferently
The seaborne to helplessness
And plays ghost from trinity
Upon those it need not bless.

It is never at once a wheel—
This succession of points in round
Which flash toward hull and keel.

Still it has to swing overground
To swing at all and agree
With required shape of earth
And how life and death must be
And love and birth.

To Earth

I died but woke again
Lying on summer ground
Looking up through a tree
At sunlight in green leaves
Where speckle-dappled birds
Played the black branches.

When I was very young
I learned how black can shine
By husking beady seeds
Out of columbine pods:
Black mica or birds' eyes
Are not a shinier black.

Consider, furthermore,
That these are seeds outwhispering
Dry, dead urns—
And poured into the earth
Will ascend again
And descend like doves

In white and purple clusters
Every next spring's sun
Hovering like small doves;

That Harlequin also
Is dappled: lives and dies
And lives—like us—and laughs.

Looking up through the tree
I saw all shining sun
Intermittent with leaves
No less than the bird-song
And buttress-branched across
As I had loved it most.

Bermuda Suite

1: *The Voyage*

The gray the vacant circle of the sea
Port and starboard sways among the clouds.
Like a slow metronome for timelessness
The centered ship creaks deeply down the east
Then slides against the west to tilt on clouds
That hold all this lolling quicksilver.

And thus eternity except for us;
Though keeled and waked obliterative in foam
Our interceptions of this pulsing void
Grew its existence and inhabitants,
And with salt tongue and all-pervading eye
Named the pastures of leviathan.

Marked by multitudinous hoofs of the wind
The waters of the world before the world
Have now become the landless skyless world,

And gray and cold and dumb and meaningless
Save for the mastery of our prow, and that
Advancing always rolls dead center still.

Southeast where morning showed beyond the prow,
Only the intermittent flaws in cloud—
Which mend and darken with a chilling zeal—
Admit light's vibrant archipelagoes.
Their brief creations on the ocean flash
Like glittering ghostly islands of the sun.

2: *The Green Moray*

Fourteen miles off the land the sharp reefs fissure the water
    and at low-tide the water splits white on the coral bone;
None does, but a man could walk here.
What lurks here, deep and obscure in the swilling waters, is
    the great eel, the green moray.

This reef-arch, vertebrae revealed, locked skeletons where the
    volcanic spew shuddering away failed northwest to achieve
One island more,—
This guards the Eden of hibiscus, floating Bermudas, crescent
    of strung barges of flowers between the cobalt air and the
    zircon-melted sea.
All those islands in a dust of gold
Strewing on water their harebell-haunted hills
That change from morning to evening from blue to mauve,
Staked with cedar, paved with lily, branched with palm, and
    breathing freesia
Under the singing rings of scarlet birds.

Toward those the green moray lifts an indifferent eye long-
    learned in patient hate; slow and watchful amidst coral
Shifts the thick mass of his cold length;

Coiled in the dead defenses of the reefs he waits vicious for
    millennium,
When from the grottoes worms the landward march of the
    fathom-hidden,
Innumerable in a sluggish final seminal wave.

3: *Portrait of Lizards*

The lizard on the limestone wall
Shifts a noncommittal eye,
Innocently prehistorical.

Miss Moore remarked his heavy clay:
Miniature dinosaurian,
Ownerless, immortal toy.

Rust on cedar, blue on stone,
Green-mottle to the yucca spikes,
He poses frozen in the sun.

All afternoon is how he likes
Baking on his chilly buff:
So we assume: that what it takes

To stay so everlasting tough
Is thus desiring heat and light
While never getting quite enough.

He has not climbed far from the sight
And sound and savor of the sea,
Yet he has compromised the night

With undivulged facility.
He scuttles where the cacti sprawl
Across the rock; amidst them, he

Mounts a dome of brain coral:
There, self-fixed, triumphant, small,
The lizard's portrait of a moral . . .

Cold, chameleon, inexplicable.

4: Kites, Good Friday

Upon mine honor, sir, I heard a humming,
And that a strange one too, which did awake me.
                              —The Tempest

Seven little boys like silhouettes dancing far on the headland
Salute the morning with the running and the rising of their
          kites.
                    Uphill, drawing them, the soft brown hands
          paying out string,
The boys have set them swinging in the wind on a rag-tailed
          rocking and rising
And riding with a surge higher and east toward the sun and out on
Tauter string over the sea—far—stretched—rigid now—
          anchored and almost stilled
Stiffly balancing wind: each octagonal kite like a burning gem
Purple and gold and red; seal-centered with—invisibly—the
          bright paper heart;
The humming beginning now out of the strung-wedged V's, a
          high keening across the Good Friday sun;
And cries on and on.

                    Swiftly by ancient custom all over the
          Bermuda islands
The sky fills—thousands of many-colored kites staining like
          marvels of windows the great blue air.
The sky sways with the glass of God, the whole dome throbbing
          with massed fretting of jewels, and their crying

Motored now to a diapason pulse, a humming roar drowning the
    wind;
And looped over the white shores and the outer reefs the foams
Break without sound.

                 In this blazing dazzle of color
    all heaven moans
Reels in this spangling of spectrum; the air imbued
Purple and gold and red: ascending and singing day-dream strung
From the thousands of soft hands that have set sounding together
Multitudinous wires, space-filling harp tilting its mineral
    fires slant to the sun,
All fragmented are joined and woven, transformed, and the sky
    opening with transfigured blood.

Between all lifted hands and the kites such intense power strains,
Which holds? Which is held?
The power flows up the strings into the sky out of the hands
    that have set this glory there,
All faces lifted to love what they have made.
Even all the islands for this little while
Lifted between the waters and the sky.

              5: Long. 64°50′W; Lat. 32°15′N

Flared down from broken cloud the calipered light
Stood strident, made exact embrace of land.
Brooched crescent upon platinum the islands
Curved gold-flecked emerald, and there was light
Only along the great bow of the islands
As though they swung burning alone in space.

Running out of the sea the man and woman
Flashed on the shore naked and beautiful,
And flung to sand as by a wave of air

They lay together breathlessly and then
They heard their hearts, and time resumed its beat.
Sand kept flickering with the ticking wind.

The sand swept high to a long wave of earth
That, wrought upon the rock, had rooted rock
Tendrilled in a gigantic grasp from air
Holding in perilous suspension
What cragged mass the sea once lifted up,
Conjoined from accident this miracle.

At its emergent line the man and woman
Stared at cloud-vexed sky, the chains of light.
They saw the flowered headlands shake and quiet
In crisscross hammering of their sea-lashed hearts,
And remembered in wild wonder-eaten wisdom
That all the flowering was meant for them.

Coleridge

Old father, blessed ghost, mariner
Of my launching, fixer of the bloody sun
Round which my condemned and lifelong voyage
Swerves and follows—follows again, ignorant
What tropic oceans, what icy straits
Hide ahead, or winds across the magnet
Shudder deeper than engines, or tides
Trouble the ways before the invisible pole
Set under that unsetting sun;

                    old talker
Glittering through my childhood—voice and eyes

Compellent to hold, to send me out to
Find home by way of Vinland, India, by
Horns of undiscovered coasts that sounded
Music undeniable till the sea
Flamed with mirage that grayed all gold;

                                        old
Detective of death in the boy's hand in the lane—
Resolve my life again. By this invocation
Invoke me—blessed ghost, old father.

INDEX TO TITLES

INDEX TO FIRST LINES